African Grey Parrot, *Psittacus erithacus erithacus.*

Photo Credits: Dr. Herbert R. Axelrod; Glen Axelrod; David Alderton; Joan Balzarini; Louise Bauck; T.Brosset; Dr. E.W.Burr; Michael DeFreitas; John Daniel; Isabelle Francais; Michael Gilroy; A.Hannson; S.W.Hutchinson; A. Jesse; B.Kahl; Horst Mayer; Louise Van der Meid; E.J.Mulawka; Robert Pearcy

Distributed in the UNITED STATES to the Pet Trade by T.F.H. Publications, Inc., One T.F.H. Plaza, Neptune City, NJ 07753; distributed in the UNITED STATES to the Bookstore and Library Trade by National Book Network, Inc. 4720 Boston Way, Lanham MD 20706; in CANADA to the Pet Trade by H & L Pet Supplies Inc., 27 Kingston Crescent, Kitchener, Ontario N2B 2T6; Rolf C. Hagen Ltd., 3225 Sartelon Street, Montreal 382 Quebec; in CANADA to the Book Trade by Vanwell Publishing Ltd., 1 Northrup Crescent, St. Catharines, Ontario L2M 6P5 ; in ENGLAND by T.F.H. Publications, PO Box 15, Waterlooville PO7 6BQ; in AUSTRALIA AND THE SOUTH PACIFIC by T.F.H. (Australia), Pty. Ltd., Box 149, Brookvale 2100 N.S.W., Australia; in NEW ZEALAND by Brooklands Aquarium Ltd. 5 McGiven Drive, New Plymouth, RD1 New Zealand; in Japan by T.F.H. Publications, Japan—Jiro Tsuda, 10-12-3 Ohjidai, Sakura, Chiba 285, Japan; in SOUTH AFRICA by Lopis (Pty) Ltd., P.O. Box 39127, Booysens, 2016, Johannesburg, South Africa. Published by T.F.H. Publications, Inc.
MANUFACTURED IN THE UNITED STATES OF AMERICA
BY T.F.H. PUBLICATIONS, INC.

Keeping
AFRICAN GREY PARROTS

Adult African Grey Parrot, *Psittacus erithacus erithacus.*

DAVID ALDERTON
TS-111

No other parrot compares to the African Grey. Its colors are unique, and no species comes close to its powers of mimicry.

Contents

Grey Parrots are highly coordinated. They can easily hold an object, such as this branch, in one foot, and balance themselves on the other.

INTRODUCING AFRICAN GREY PARROTS

The African Grey Parrot is probably the best-known parrot in the world. These parrots have been kept as pets for centuries in the villages of its native range, northern-central Africa. The date of their introduction to Europe is unclear. It is certain that they were known there as long ago as the 1500s, since in England, one was a favored pet of King Henry VIII (1509-1547). This parrot resided at his palace, Hampton Court, just outside London, and soon learned to call the ferryman across the water!

This link with royalty appears to have been maintained over successive centuries. An African Grey kept by a mistress of Charles II (1661-1685) was actually buried with her in Westminster Abbey. It is now accepted as the oldest surviving example of avian taxidermy. Then, during the reign of Queen Victoria (1837-1901), an African Grey Parrot christened "Coco" lived at her residence at Sandringham in Norfolk. Among its phrases was the loyal statement "God save the Queen!"

For many years, the African Grey has been seen largely as an intelligent companion bird. Today, many more of these parrots are being kept for breeding purposes, rather than just as pets. It is quite common to raise their chicks from the egg by hand. This has proved to be a significant advance because not all pairs make reliable parents. Furthermore, Greys are relatively quiet birds, compared with other parrots of similar size such as the Amazons (genus *Amazona*). This makes them much more suitable occupants of an outside aviary in a fairly urbanized area where close neighbors could object to the birds' calls.

The Grey's power of mimicry is probably unsurpassed by any other member of the parrot family. This, of course, has led to its

The darker tail feathers of the Timneh Grey Parrot are easily distinguishable from the bright red coloration of the nominate race.

widespread popularity. Even aviary birds have been taught to talk successfully.

Grey Parrots are instantly recognizable; they have gray body coloration and bright red tails. Their unusual color scheme is unique among parrots. Indeed, the only other predominantly gray colored parrots are the two species of Vasa Parrot (genus *Coracopsis*), found on Madagascar and other neighboring islands off the south-west coast of Africa.

In both cases, these are a darker shade of gray, bordering on black, and possess a strong brownish tinge to their plumage. Vasa Parrots show no trace of red in their tails which are also much longer than that of the African Grey, with its broad, short tail.

Anatomical studies have revealed there to be no evident link between Vasa Parrots and the African Grey. In spite of its wide distribution, the Grey Parrot appears to have no close relatives. It is therefore classified in its own genus *Psittacus*, with the species name of *erithacus* describing its red tail. The African Grey has been known to scientists much longer than many other parrots, and was first officially classified in 1758, by the famous naturalist Carolus Linnaeus.

Through the extensive range of this parrot, slight variations in appearance can be detected. In cases where the distinction is sufficiently marked, these populations have been further divided into separate races, or subspecies. The most significant race, from an avicultural viewpoint, is the Timneh Grey Parrot, *Psittacus erithacus timneh*.

This can be easily recognized by its dark maroon, rather than bright red, tail feathers. As a result of its duller appearance, these particular Grey Parrots are invariably less expensive than red-tailed birds, but prove equally competent as mimics.

It seems likely that the Grey Parrot is most closely allied to the members of the *Poicephalus* genus. The nine species in this grouping are widely distributed across much of Africa. They vary quite noticeably in both size and coloration, and include such well-known avicultural subjects as the Senegal Parrot (*P. senegalus*) and Meyer's Parrot (*P. meyeri*). The largest member of the genus is the Cape Parrot (*P. robustus*), which, at about 33 cm (13 in) in length, is of equivalent size to the Grey Parrot itself. All *Poicephalus* parrots have short, square tails, with unfeathered ceres including the nostrils, located above their powerful beaks, like the Grey Parrot. A shared ancestry with these parrots could be established if fertile eggs were produced from a Grey Parrot paired with a member of the *Poicephalus*

genus. This would confirm that they were sufficiently similar, in a genetic sense, to produce hybrid offspring. The Cape Parrot would appear to be most suitable for an experiment of this type, but it is itself very rare in aviculture. Until such time as further research of this type is carried out, the precise relationships of the Grey Parrot remain unclear.

COLORATION

The distinctive coloration of the Grey Parrot results from a partial lack of one of the two major groups of color

Grey Parrots use their beaks, as well as their feet, to clamber about their cage and surroundings.

called spongy layer, where there is no pigment, but light passing through here can be reflected back to create blue coloration in the absence of carotenoid pigments above. In the case of the Grey Parrot, the carotenoid pigments are notably absent from the body plumage, apart from the tail. Under normal circumstances, this would create a blue-colored bird, however, the spongy layer is dramatically reduced in size and can no longer reflect back blue light. The resulting effect is the creation of gray plumage in this instance.

pigment from its plumage. The majority of psittacine birds have two different types of pigments: carotenoid and melanin. Carotenoid pigments are responsible for the wide range of coloration from pale yellow through to deep red, whereas melanin is a dark pigment, associated with brown, gray, and black feathering.

These two classes of pigment are located at different levels within the feather barbs. The carotenoid group occur in the outer area, known as the cortex, while melanin is confined to the inner medulla. Separating these two regions is the so-

The depth of gray coloration varies through the Grey Parrot's distribution. Birds from the western part of the range are overall darker than those occurring in more southerly areas. Those from the Cameroons and the Congo are generally the lightest, and also the largest. They are a very pale gray and are often advertised as "silvers."

Although it is generally not possible to sex Grey Parrots reliably by visual means, you can often do so with these lighter-colored birds, assuming that they are from the same area. This is because one of the sexual characteristics of mature cock birds is increased melanin deposition in the plumage, compared to the hens. While this tends not to be obvious in the darker Grey Parrots, it is often quite evident in the so-called silvers.

Look particularly at the wings when you are seeking a breeding pair of these Greys, and choose those with the darkest wings first: they will invariably be cocks, whereas paler-winged individuals are likely to prove hens. This distinction is only evident once the birds have molted into adult plumage. There is always a possibility, therefore, that paler individuals could be immature cocks rather than hens. Confirmation of sex can be achieved by other means which will be discussed later.

COLOR VARIANTS

On occasions, Grey Parrots showing variable amounts of salmon-pink plumage among their normal gray feathering have been reported. The cause of this abnormal appearance is likely to be a defect in the metabolic

Young (nominate race) Grey Parrots develop their bright red tail feathers at about six weeks of age. They do, however, have a dark tip that does not change until the bird's first molt.

As part of the mating ritual, a bonded pair of Grey Parrots will feed each other several times a day.

pathway which leads to the synthesis of the melanin pigment from the amino acid residue called tyrosine. This change can be transitory, appearing at one molt and vanishing at the next, or else may alter in extent.

In the early 1920s, the famous aviculturist Dr. Jean Delacour owned a Grey Parrot which was almost totally pink, except for a very few odd gray feathers over its body. The coloration of this bird was described as being like that of a flamingo, with a red tail, and dark eyes and legs. It was apparently a hen, and laid five eggs, but no similarly-colored offspring were recorded.

In contrast, the "yellow" form of the Grey Parrot is probably a genuine mutation which, if bred in a similar fashion to other recessive mutations of this type, could be produced over successive generations. This would entail mating offspring back to the original mutant parent in order to test this theory. A percentage of these second generation chicks should then resemble the original mutant in appearance.

The "yellow" Grey Parrot is sometimes incorrectly described as the "albino." These birds have pure white plumage, contrasting with their bright red tails. By definition, however, an albino has no pigment present, so the tail should also be white, rather than red. The reason that the remainder of the plumage is white rather than yellow is simply that no carotenoid pigment is present here, so with melanin absent, this area of the body therefore appears white.

Another color change which is less well-documented, but more often seen, is most common in Timneh Greys. The body plumage of some of these birds is notably brownish, rather than dark gray. This change probably results from alteration to the usual melanin pigment, creating what is in effect a cinnamon variant. The

African Greys are very delicate in their eating habits. They will hold an item in their foot and take small bites, as if savoring every piece.

coloration in this instance does not appear to alter over successive molts. Further study, involving trial pairings, would probably reveal that this is a sex-linked recessive mutation, like other cinnamon mutations recorded in members of the parrot family. The depth of brown coloration can be quite variable between individuals.

MAKING A PURCHASE

While obtaining a young bird is essential for those seeking a Grey Parrot as a pet, breeders usually prefer to purchase mature individuals. The eyes play an important part in recognizing an immature Grey Parrot. Up until five months old, the eyes appear totally blackish because the iris surrounding each pupil is itself dark gray. These gradually change from about this point onwards and lighten, so that by around nine months of age, Grey Parrots have obtained the characteristic pale yellowish-white irises associated with adult birds.

It will take several years, however, before they will actually be sufficiently mature to start nesting in earnest. Most Grey Parrots are unlikely to breed before they are three years old. Purchasing recently imported mature birds does not guarantee instant success either because they require time to settle down in their new quarters.

It is very difficult to determine the age of older Greys once their irises have assumed adult coloration. They may even continue to deepen somewhat in color up to the age of about four years old, which may prove useful in distinguishing young adults. The Grey Parrot is normally a long-lived bird, with a life-expectancy of well over half a century.

When you are considering obtaining a Grey Parrot, remember that hand-raised youngsters invariably command a much higher price than imported birds. If you have no previous experience of hand-raising, do not be tempted to obtain an unweaned individual at a discount. This may prove a source of concern, especially since the weaning phase can be most difficult for the inexperienced owner.

Before deciding on a particular individual, watch the birds on offer for a few moments. They should appear lively and alert. Any which are apparently asleep, with their heads tucked back over their wings, and resting on both feet may be unwell, especially if they are not keen to move when approached. Healthy parrots usually roost by gripping the perch with one foot at a time, although recently-fledged chicks may rest with their eyes closed and support themselves on both feet.

Always check the food pot, and the bird's droppings. This should indicate first, that the parrot is eating normally, as shown by the presence of seed husks, and secondly that it is not suffering from any

When choosing a pet Grey Parrot, it is best to select only one bird. Two birds would keep each other company; however, they would pay attention to each other rather than you.

digestive upset. The droppings themselves should be well-formed, and not excessively loose, being a mixture of white and green in color. The white component corresponds to the bird's urinary output. Any indication of blood or significant discoloration of the fecal matter is potentially serious, and such birds are likely to be unwell.

If you are contemplating the purchase of a tame bird, allow the vendor to show you how the parrot will feed from the hand. Then see if the bird accepts food from you in a similar way. Greys are relatively shy by nature, and often will not follow their usual routine in close proximity to a stranger. Certainly, be sure to check out this aspect before undertaking a closer examination which may upset the parrot for a short period. Young birds will adapt to a new owner much more readily than adults.

Look closely at the eyes:

Ask your pet shop clerk to show you how a Grey Parrot will accept food from the hand. Then see if the bird will accept it from you in the same manner.

these should be clear and bright, with no staining evident on the surrounding feathering. Also check the nostrils: a minor infection here is not uncommon in Grey Parrots, and over a period of time, this may lead to an enlargement of one nostril over the other. The outer surface of the nostril can also sometimes appear blocked, or there may be a slight discharge evident, both of which indicate a problem of this type. Such infections will often flare up when the bird is placed under stress, by being moved to a new environment for example. They may also be difficult to treat successfully, often recurring at intervals.

Feather condition is especially important if you are thinking of purchasing a tame, talking bird. This is because Grey Parrots are susceptible to feather-plucking, and may pull out large areas of plumage. Although these feathers will start to regrow over a period of time, the parrot is likely to remove these as they appear, with the problem rapidly becoming habitual. This can prove a very difficult situation to remedy successfully. If the bird on offer has only a thin covering of feathers, or even clear bald patches on its chest or abdomen, this needs to be considered seriously. A recently-imported parrot may have the feathers of one wing clipped, preventing it from flying effectively. In the surroundings of a cage, this will not prove an undue handicap, but in an aviary, there is a risk that the bird could fall to the floor and injure itself internally, if it was suddenly frightened, by a cat leaping onto the structure for example. Be prepared to screen the aviary as much as possible under these circumstances, and

A lot can be told about a bird's personality from its eyes. An angry or nasty Grey will constrict its pupils and growl like a dog.

Grey Parrots have the ability to mimic many different words and phrases. They will even compile a group of gurgles and whistles on their own.

provide a soft floor covering. The feathers should soon be molted, and then your parrot will be able to fly without difficulty.

It is also useful to obtain an indication of the bird's bodily condition by checking its breast bone. This can be found running from the lower chest to the abdomen. It should be just palpable in a parrot in good condition. However, if the bird appears healthy in all other respects, there is no need for undue concern

if this bone is slightly more prominent. Weight loss can be a feature of several long-term avian diseases such as aspergillosis. If the bird appears potentially poor in other respects, by having plumage which is fluffed up, or breathing noisily, it is best avoided.

Finally, check that there is no fecal contamination of the feathering around the vent, which is often a sign of a digestive disorder. It is also important that the feet appear normal, and show no swelling or paralysis of the individual toes. Such a condition would otherwise handicap the parrot's ability to perch normally.

The purchase of a Grey Parrot is a costly undertaking. Pet stores are now offering their birds with health certificates supplied by veterinarians. In addition, surgically-sexed Grey Parrots (often advertised with the initials "S.S."), may be banded, enabling the cock and hen to be identified individually from the certificate. Alternatively, they may be marked with a micro-chip implant, which affords greater protection against theft. This is because the tiny implant is actually located in the bird's body, and the encoded number

Grey Parrots pair bond for life. Very often if a pair is separated, each bird will not accept a new mate because it will long to have back the original.

is totally unique, being read using a special scanner.

You will probably have to pay more for a confirmed pair of Greys, but this does not guarantee their compatibility. As reliable sexing methods have become widely-used, so it is now increasingly apparent that Grey Parrots do have individual preferences when it comes to choosing a mate. The ideal, but most expensive way of obtaining a breeding pair is still to purchase several birds (6-8), and allow them to pair off themselves. The chances of obtaining a compatible pair are greatly enhanced by this means. Alternatively, you may wish to seek out a proven pair, although these often command a premium price.

HOUSING AFRICAN GREY PARROTS

A cage for a Grey Parrot should provide the bird with plenty of room to exercise. There are many different styles and sizes available from your local pet shop.

Even if you plan to keep your Grey Parrot in an aviary, it is advisable to obtain a suitable cage for it to be placed in first. This is because the bird will need to settle down in its new surroundings, and its behavior can be monitored more easily than if it is placed in a large enclosure. Imported Greys, although having undergone their period of quarantine, will not be acclimatized in any event. They should not be transferred outdoors unless the weather is certain to remain mild for a number of weeks ahead.

Your local pet store will be able to offer you a range of cages suitable to your new pet. Choose a large enclosure, especially if this is intended to be the parrot's permanent home. A rectangular or square design is preferred; Greys do not thrive in circular cages. They often display signs of behavioral stress in these surroundings, such as repeated head-weaving. In addition, many parrots like to sit on top of their cage when they are permitted to do so. The domed roof of circular cages is less satisfactory for this purpose.

A cage at least 75cm (30in) square is recommended for a Grey

Parrot. Perches made of natural or fresh-cut tree branches are best for birds. These provide a variable thickness necessary for the birds to exercise their feet. Only use non-poisonous woods, such as branches cut from apple or sycamore trees, and be certain that these have not been previously sprayed with insecticides. It is a good idea to also scrub them, just in case they were contaminated by the droppings of wild birds. Do not use old, dead branches which could be affected by fungus, as this is likely to be harmful to the parrot.

Grey Parrots enjoy sitting on top of their cage. They feel secure because it is their home, yet enjoy it because they are given freedom.

cleaning. This should be at least 1.25cm (.5in) in depth, preferably more, so that dirt such as seed husks cannot become jammed here when you clean out the cage. Metal trays are not likely to be chewed by the parrot, unlike those made of plastic, but check that there are no gaps where the parrot's claws could become caught at the edges of the folded metal sheeting. Most cages are equipped with food pots which can be refilled from the outside. It is best to purchase a separate drinking container for your parrot. This will guarantee the bird with plenty of food pots and a constant supply of fresh, clean water.

Many owners use just plain, uncolored newspaper to line the floor of the cage, but this tends to be unsightly. Your local pet shop will carry various proprietary floor coverings. Shavings which are free from toxic wood preservatives are another popular covering available from pet stores that prove to be an excellent absorbent.

Many of the bigger and more attractive cages available today are mounted on a stand that can be moved quite easily

Feed cups that are accessible from the outside of your pet's cage make caring for your pet a lot easier.

You will need a cage with a secure door fastening. Greys are intelligent parrots, and can soon work out how to undo most simple latches. They use their tongues as well as their beaks for this purpose. A small padlock is not a bad idea and it can be fastened to the cage door as an added security measure.

The majority of cages are equipped with a sliding tray to facilitate on castors. This makes the task of cleaning around the cage much easier, and you will not need to have a large piece of furniture in the room to stand the cage on. Try to avoid positioning the cage in the center of the room. Choose a spot preferably in a corner. This will give the parrot a greater feeling of security, so it will be less stressed in its new surroundings. If the bird feels threatened here it can withdraw to the back of its cage, rather than being accessible from all sides.

OUTDOOR ACCOMMODATION

Even if you intend to keep your parrots in an aviary, it is useful to have several spare cages available. You may, at some time, purchase birds which cannot be transferred immediately outdoors, and cages always prove to be useful temporary accommodation. The traditional aviary design, comprising of an outside flight connected to a shed-like shelter, is ideal for Grey Parrots, provided it is adapted and strengthened to resist their beaks.

BUILDING A FLIGHT

The framework for the flight should be constructed of timber which is 5cm (2in) square. The size of the flight is obviously influenced by the space available. Overall, a pair of Greys would thrive in an aviary of 3.6m (12ft)

The bars of a Grey Parrot's cage must be of a stout gauge so that the bird's powerful beak cannot destroy it.

long, 1.8m (6ft) high and 1m (3ft) wide. It helps to build the frames around the dimensions of the mesh which will be used to cover them. This saves time, and avoids unnecessary cutting and wastage of the mesh. You will need 16 gauge (G) mesh for Grey Parrots, since they will be able to destroy thinner, 19G wire mesh. If you decide to purchase ready-made aviary panels, check that the correct thickness of mesh is used to cover them. The spacing between the individual strands of wire in the mesh is also important to keep vermin and snakes out of the aviary. They may otherwise spread disease and harm

to the parrots. Snakes will even eat young chicks in the nest box if they can gain access here. To protect the birds, avoid using mesh with individual strand spacings of more than 2.5 x 1.25cm (1 x .5in).

The timber to be used for the framework of the aviary should be treated with a non-toxic, weather-proofing agent. This is easier to carry out before you assemble the lengths into panels. It should be possible to obtain the timber already cut into the appropriate lengths, so you can either fix the lengths together, or join them for a more stable structure.

When you are ready to

apply the aviary mesh over the framework, lay the frame down on a level surface. Then carefully unroll the mesh over the full face, anchoring it in place at first with netting staples at the top. Run the mesh over the whole of the frame, so that once assembled, none of the timber will be accessible to the parrots. This protects the woodwork from their beaks. Always allow a slight overlap at the top and bottom of each frame, so that when the mesh is cut, you can knock down the sharp strands onto the adjoining face. In this way, when the panels are fixed together there will be no loose ends of wire in the flight which could injure the parrots.

It helps if you have someone else to hold the mesh while you are cutting it, and actually fixing it to the frame. They can keep the mesh taut and square on the frame, leaving you free to concentrate on tacking the mesh in position. Space netting staples about every 5cm (2in) around the framework, and be sure to drive these soundly into the timber. Grey Parrots often spend long periods climbing around their aviary, and can get a claw caught if there is a gap

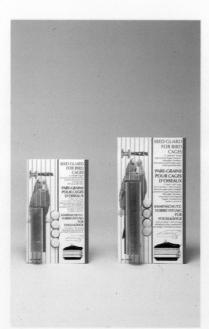

Grey Parrots can be messy birds, and seed guards help to keep some of the debris inside the cage. Your local pet shop will carry one to fit your specific cage. Photo courtesy of Hagen Products.

between the mesh and netting staple.

If you are planning to include a door in the aviary flight, make the frame and cover it with mesh, but do not fix it into the flight panel until the structure is assembled and nearly completed.

SITE PREPARATION

Choose a spot in the backyard which is reasonably sheltered, but not overhung by trees. Wild birds perching here are otherwise likely to contaminate the aviary with their droppings, presenting a hazard to the parrots within. Also, branches may break off in a storm, damaging the aviary, and leaves will accumulate on the roof in the fall.

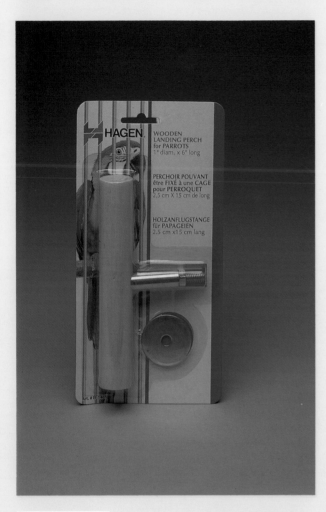

serve to deter casual vandalism, and more deliberate thieving, which unfortunately is becoming increasingly common as the value of parrots continues to rise. In addition, the headlights of passing vehicles may disturb the birds after dark. This can be devastating during the breeding period.

The amount of preparation required depends on your soil, and the climate. In areas where high winds are a regular occurrence, specific building regulations may apply to the construction of aviaries. It is also important to check with your local planning office to ensure that no formal application is needed before starting to build the aviary. A simple plan of your backyard, with the position and dimensions of the aviary marked, will be helpful for this purpose. Before starting work in earnest, clear the site and cut out turf carefully. If this is then rolled up and kept in the shade, you can use it again later around the base of the aviary. It also saves the need to sow grass seed, giving a more finished appearance to the structure.

Sitting on top of a cage is made more comfortable for a Grey Parrot with a landing perch. Your pet shop dealer can demonstrate the ease with which this can attach to any cage. Just ask! Photo courtesy of Hagen Products.

It is also better if the aviary is approached from the front, rather than around the sides. Greys can be nervous parrots, and this approach allows them to retreat to the back of the flight, rather than flying up and down the aviary. Obviously, a quiet location is preferred, away from a children's play area for example.

The aviary also needs to be hidden from the road as far as possible. This will

Mark out the precise dimensions carefully. Then prepare the footings which will ultimately support the aviary framework. Blocks set at least 30cm (12in) below ground level in a trench around the perimeter, and for a similar distance above, are ideal for the purpose. You can then face them externally with mortar, and paint the base to create an attractive finish once the aviary is in place.

It is essential to have assistance when you fix the frames in place, although this can now be achieved quite easily using frame-fixers, which are passed through the timber into the block work beneath. Choose frame-fixers of adequate length to anchor the timber firmly in place. The panels

Paneling that is used inside of a bird's aviary is sure to be chewed apart. However, it is very much enjoyed and is safe—as long as you do not mind replacing it every so often.

themselves can be joined together in a similar fashion, or using nuts and bolts. Be sure to include washers as well, and keep the bolts well-greased so that if you need to dismantle the aviary later, you can do so easily, and move it without causing any unnecessary damage to the structure.

BUILDING THE SHELTER

Grey Parrots are quite hardy once properly acclimatized, but they will need dry, draft-proof roosting quarters attached to the flight. This framework should be constructed sectionally like the flight, but it will need to be covered on its outer face with thick external plywood, or tongued-and-grooved wood.

In either case, the interior of the shelter will need to be lined with aviary mesh, in order to prevent the parrots from damaging the interior with their beaks. Windows should also be covered, in case the parrots try to fly through the glass, and injure themselves.

The shelter must be well-lit or otherwise the parrots will prefer to roost in the flight at night. It is therefore a good idea to include a window on one side of the shelter, and also another at the back set into a

Your pet Grey Parrot wil enjoy swinging in its cage. A pet shop near you will carry a variety of swings to suit the type of bird you keep. Photo courtesy of Hagen Products.

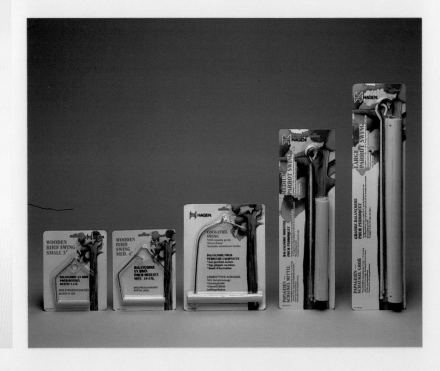

door. There are obviously several variations as to where you can include doors around the aviary, but a door at the back of the shelter is most useful. Here, you can enter directly to feed the parrots undercover, and do not have to walk through the flight and disturb them especially when they may be breeding.

PREVENTING AN ESCAPE

It is best to include a safety porch at the back of the shelter. Here it will be less conspicuous than if sited at the front of the aviary. The safety porch, usually 90cm (3 ft) square, simply serves to ensure that the parrots cannot escape when you enter the aviary. It can be built on identical lines to the flight, but must include a door which opens outwards. Before you go into the aviary it is important that you remember to close this behind you, and secure it with a bolt. The aviary door can then be opened knowing that if a parrot does slip by you, it will remain confined in the safety porch. Once the bird has flown back into the aviary, and you want to leave the shelter, this double-door system will again prevent accidental escapes if you simply close the shelter door

When moved outside, Grey Parrots should not be left unsupervised. They become easy targets for neighborhood dogs and cats which could inflict a nasty wound!

Suspended flights are becoming more popular among bird keepers. They help to keep the birds in a more hygienic condition because their droppings fall right to the floor.

first. In order for the system to work easily, however, this particular door must be hinged to open in the direction of the shelter's interior.

This arrangement within an African Grey aviary is most satisfactory. Entry to the flight itself, which will probably only be needed about once a week or so for cleaning purposes, is through a connecting door, which should open outwards, from the shelter.

PROTECTING THE WOODWORK

Since the front of the shelter here is accessible to the parrots on both sides, it is vital to protect the external face from their beaks as much as possible. A solid sheet of plywood should be used for cladding here, since tongued-and-grooved wood provides a greater area for the parrots to gnaw, in comparison to a flat surface.

Where there are exposed edges, notably around the door, be sure to avoid placing perches nearby, which could allow the parrots to have easy access to the woodwork. A combination of careful screening, and an ample supply of fresh perches for the birds, should ensure that the aviary framework is not unduly damaged over a period of time. Although some breeders use flat strips of tin tacked over exposed edges, this tends to have sharp edges, which could slice into a parrot's fleshy tongue.

A Grey Parrot confined to a cage, will enjoy the time it spends away from this. It will, upon being let out, take several minutes to stretch and exercise.

Shiny, noisy, and fun... toy bells for birds are available from your local pet shop for all sized birds. Photo courtesy of Hagen Products.

An access hatch for the parrots will also need to be included at the front of the shelter, with a platform, so they can land here easily. This is usually quite high up, and can be fitted as part of the door. Position this carefully so that the platform does not interfere with the opening of the door if it comes into contact with the side of the flight. You can add vertical sides around the platform. These will help to keep the shelter free from drafts.

ROOFING

The components of the shelter will need to be assembled on similar lines to that of the flight, but you will need to decide, before starting work, on the shape of the roof. Although an apex roof can be used, it is often easier to construct a sloping flat roof, adjusting the height of the sides accordingly so the water will run off away from the flight. The rear of the shelter therefore needs to be built to a lower level than that of the front.

An overhang of several inches of the roof means that rain will not soak back, but rather will be channeled off. The easiest means of covering the roof is to use a double layer of roofing felt. Although mineralized roofing felt is more expensive, it usually proves more durable than plain felt, which splits readily when constantly exposed to temperature changes, and sunlight. Plastic guttering can also be fixed along the back and sides of the roof, to collect run-off of rainwater, channeling it away.

FLOORING

The floor of the aviary can be finished in several ways. Although a covering

Opposite page: A Grey Parrot will not give up a favored food or treat easily. It will hold onto it even while it is disturbed.

Below: Toys sometimes frustrate Greys, but that's half of the fun! It is often just as much fun for an owner to watch his pet play as it is for the pet at play!

Grey Parrots that are residents of outdoor aviaries enjoy the sunshine and fresh air. The aviary must, however, have some sort of roofing to protect the birds from too much sun and from pouring rain.

of grass will be attractive in the flight, this is rarely practical, unless you have a large aviary. Otherwise, the grass dies off quite readily, and it will be difficult to keep the floor clean. At the other extreme, a concrete floor covering can be hosed and scrubbed off as necessary, but it looks relatively unattractive. This is certainly, however, the covering of choice for the shelter, where seed husks will be spilt. You will then need to cover just the floor with several layers of newspaper, and replace these as necessary.

As an alternative to concrete in the outside flight, you can use a thick layer of coarse gravel at least 22.5cm (9in) in depth, setting paving slabs beneath the perches where

the majority of droppings will accumulate. You will then be able to scrape off the slabs, and just rake over the gravel at intervals, removing feathers from the surface by hand. Drainage can sometimes be a problem with this option, particularly in areas of heavy rainfall.

Always allow for drainage from the flight by sloping a concrete floor to a small exit hole close to the base, and making a similar slope when compacting the floor and covering it with gravel. You may prefer to combine the advantages of concrete with the less permanent option of gravel, by laying paving slabs over the whole graveled area, and filling between them with mortar. Drainage under these conditions can be more difficult to achieve, and it may be worth seeking the help of a professional builder to complete this task.

PERCHES

The perches for the parrots will need to be positioned across rather than along the aviary. The birds will then be able to fly up and down without difficulty. Generally, you will need two main perches running across the flight at opposite ends, allowing

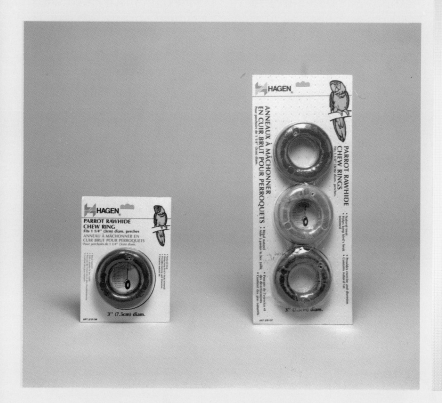

Since parrots love to chew so much, why not make it fun and exciting! Rawhide chew rings can be purchased from your local pet shop in a variety of colors. Photo courtesy of Hagen Products.

Natural, non-toxic tree branches should be included inside a cage or aviary.

Tonic and mineral blocks contain a variety of necessary minerals which birds find in their natural environment. Available from pet shops everywhere. Photo courtesy of Hagen Products.

adequate clearance for the parrots to turn around without any difficulty. Two or three perches will also be needed in the shelter to give easy access to the food and water containers here if these are not located at ground level.

Branches cut from a variety of trees are suitable, but be certain they are not likely to be poisonous in any way, perhaps as a result of being treated with chemical sprays. Always wash them off, in case they have been contaminated by droppings from wild birds.

Once you have finished building the aviary, it is advisable to cover part of the outside flight, nearest the shelter, with

translucent plastic sheeting. This will provide some additional protection for the parrots if they choose to perch here during periods of bad weather. The plastic on the roof will need to be fitted so that rainwater runs off away from the shelter. You can achieve this easily by adding an additional length of timber to what will be the highest point, thus creating a downward slope of the plastic sheeting towards the end of the flight. Generally, a

All birds, especially Grey Parrots, require natural tree branches inside of their cage to gnaw upon. This is natural for the birds to do in the wild, and they should not be denied the pleasure.

Suspended breeding flights are very popular because not only are they hygienic, but the birds do not have to be disturbed during cleaning because all debris falls to the floor.

covering between 90-180cm (3-6ft) on the roof will be adequate, allowing at least one exposed perch in the aviary where the parrots can bathe easily in the rain.

OTHER OPTIONS

Apart from the traditional standard aviary, suspended flights have recently gained considerably in popularity. These are easier to clean, and have less of a disturbance to the birds, because the droppings can fall through the wire-mesh floor, out of their reach. The floor of a suspended flight is usually supported with brick pillars.

Although wire clips can be used to fix the lengths of mesh together to form the flight, a wooden framework will again result in a more stable structure. It is important to use slightly broader strands of mesh to form the floor of a suspended flight, otherwise the droppings are likely to accumulate within the structure. There they will be difficult to remove, if they do not fall through the floor. The individual dimensions of this mesh therefore need to be at least 2.5cm (1 in) square.

The shelter itself can

also be built in a suspended fashion, supported on legs. It is certainly advisable to include a full-length safety porch around the service door at the rear of the shelter. This will reduce the risk of the parrots slipping out when you feed them. You can also convert a shed or similar out building to accommodate suspended flights. Here you will be able to install a number of breeding pairs, using the sectional cages available from pet stores. These can also be adapted to form outdoor suspended flights. No shelter component is usually required for Grey Parrots housed indoors, and you can introduce artificial lighting and even heating in a bird room of this type. This particular kind of set-up offers considerable scope for the serious breeder.

An outdoor aviary may require some sort of permission from your local zoning board. Check out this aspect with your town before you get too deep into plans.

Vegetables that are offered to your
pet can be fed raw or cooked.
However, raw vegetables have a
higher vitamin content.

FEEDING AFRICAN GREY PARROTS

In the wild, African Grey Parrots have been observed feeding on a wide variety of nuts, fruits, and berries. In wooded areas, they can be difficult to pick out because they are camouflaged as they move through the treetops and climb among the branches. African Grey Parrots also descend to feed on the ground, especially in agricultural areas. In such areas, flocks can be serious pests of both ripening maize and groundnut crops.

For many years, the tendency has been to offer these parrots a diet comprised of dried seeds in the form of a standard parrot mixture. This usually contains sunflower seeds, peanuts, maize, and possibly hemp. Other ingredients such as chillies, safflower, oats, and pumpkin seeds also form part of some mixtures.

Ask at your pet store for a good quality seed mix. It is possible to buy branded mixtures, which usually offer a guarantee of consistent quality. The seed on offer should not be dusty or dirty in any way, or contain harvesting debris such as stones.

The store will also be able to provide you with suitable feeding bowls. Those made of plastic tend to be destroyed quite easily, so choose a stainless steel bowl. Some designs incorporate a screw fitting, so they can

The main constituent of a Grey Parrot's diet is seed. In addition to the seed part of a bird's diet, many fresh fruits and vegetables can also be offered.

Grey Parrots use their feet in much the same way that we use our hands. They hold objects with them to assist in eating.

be held in place on the sides of the cage or aviary mesh.

Seed containers that simply hang against the side of the cage are less satisfactory. They are often tipped over, with their contents being scattered everywhere. Heavyweight dog bowls are satisfactory containers for seed. Their weight means that the parrots will be unlikely to upturn them.

Some sort of container for drinking water will also be needed. There are many different styles available from your local pet store.

OTHER FOODS

It is now realized that dry seeds do not offer a complete balanced diet for parrots. To remain in a healthy condition they need more variety in their diet. Feather-plucking, for example, is a common problem in Grey Parrots. This can often be linked to an inadequate diet.

These birds do have individual tastes, so what appeals to one may be less appealing to another. Many different types of fresh fruits and vegetables will be well appreciated by these birds. This, combined with a good seed mixture will offer a balanced diet. Grey Parrots can be rather conservative in their feeding habits, and if they are used to a diet comprised largely of sunflower seed, it may be difficult to persuade them to sample other foods, even if these are nutritionally superior.

If you start with a young, hand-raised Grey, then you will probably find that it will soon take other foods readily. Such birds will show little of the natural reluctance of untamed adults in taking such foods.

Another recent trend in psittacine nutrition has been the use of pulses, such as mung beans, to form a regular part of birds' diet. These can be sprouted (as for human consumption), and then fed to the parrots. Be sure to wash off the sprouted seeds very thoroughly, and allow them to drain before offering them to the birds; just as you would if you were eating them.

While not all Grey Parrots will eat mung beans, they will often take soaked sunflower seed. This is usually accepted quite readily, and mung beans can be introduced by this means, mixing them in with the sunflower seeds. Choose either striped or white sunflower seed for this purpose, and not black because this releases a dye into the water, which some breeders claim can be harmful to parrots. Start as with mung beans, by washing the required amount in a colander and remove any obvious remains of stalks or other grass debris. Only use a small amount of seed, since after soaking, any remaining uneaten will have to be thrown away within a day. Soaking serves to stimulate the germination process, but at the same time, it encourages fungal growth.

Cover the seed with warm water, in a suitable bowl, and leave it to stand

A young Grey Parrot will more readily take and accept new foods than an older bird already set in its ways.

for about twenty-four hours. Then, after a thorough rinsing under a running tap, tip the seed into a heavyweight feeding bowl. Obviously, don't mix it with dried seed once it is wet.

You will need to remove the husks and any remaining seed within a few hours. It is often easiest to provide soaked seed in the morning, and then take away the remains later on during the day. This is particularly important when the weather is hot, as fungi develop more rapidly under these conditions. Although they may not cause immediate obvious harm to adult birds, fungal infections can be fatal for young chicks and may lead to liver damage in older stock.

STORING SEED

It is important to store seed in dry surroundings. Should the seed become wet, it will begin to mold. Peanuts, in particular, are prone to a dangerous fungus. Storing seed in sealed plastic sacks is not recommended, because of the risk of condensation. Sacks of any type are not really suitable out-of-doors in any event because their contents will be easily accessible to vermin. A metal dust bin is a much safer option.

If you have just one pair

Spray millet is enjoyed by all birds. This proves to be a nutritious part of every bird's diet. Available from your local pet shop in various quantities. Photo courtesy of Hagen Products.

of Grey Parrots, you will be using several pounds of seed per month. It is usually cheaper and more convenient to purchase a larger quantity. This can be stored for six months or so, without affecting its feeding value to any significant extent. The best way to check the freshness of seed is to soak a set number of sunflower seeds for example, and then see how many sprout. Old seed has a much lower level of germination.

It is best to use up one batch of seed completely before starting on a new supply. Also, clean out the storage bin thoroughly between batches, just in case fodder mites are present. The first sign of fodder mites is likely to be an uncharacteristic sweet smell having run your hands through the seed. Closer examination reveals a fine dusty powder, in which the minute mites may be visible, especially if viewed through a magnifying glass. There is no real evidence to show that fodder mites are directly harmful to parrots, but obviously they do not improve the quality of the seed.

Be sure to wash out the food bowl thoroughly, and dry it before refilling it with clean seed.

You should wash all the food pots and water containers regularly in any event. Obviously, containers used for soaked seed and other perishable foodstuffs will need to be

A Grey Parrot's beak is very powerful and can do a great deal of damage. However, the gentle nature of the bird shows as it takes items from one's hand very carefully.

Offer a good amount of a favored items to your pet parrots so that bickering does not occur over one particular thing.

cleaned daily. It can be useful to have a spare set, so that you can simply swap the pots around each day. If you use a disinfectant to clean the bowls more thoroughly, be sure to rinse them off completely. It is also advisable to do the same with a detergent.

Drinking containers must be washed and rinsed every day to prevent algal growth on the sides of the container, however, greenish deposits will still appear here. Certain algae may release harmful toxins into the water, so the container should be kept as clean as possible. On cold days, when the temperature is likely to fall below zero, avoid filling the drinking container to capacity. If the water inside freezes, it will expand, and then the container is likely to split as a result.

FRESH FOODS

Depending on where you live, it should be possible to obtain a variety of fresh fruit and green stuff for your parrots throughout the year. These are a valuable source of vitamins, and help to provide bulk without a high calorie intake. Pet Grey Parrots kept inside are especially at risk to obesity, which will shorten their life span. Fresh foods also give them interest in their food, helping to keep them occupied and away from the more fatty seeds.

Although fruit is a natural part of a wild Grey Parrot's diet, imported birds, in particular, may refuse such items at first. It will then be a matter of persevering and finding which fruits will tempt your bird.

Sweet apples are a useful starting point because they are freely-available. All fruit should be washed and the skin removed if one believes chemical residues may remain. Cut the fruit into quarters, checking that no part of it has gone bad. Only use top quality, unblemished fruit, as otherwise it might harm your bird.

Grapes are a favorite of many Grey Parrots, as are berries in season. Firm, not over-ripe bananas are also popular with some birds, but prove very messy and can be difficult to clean up, especially in the confines of a cage. Slices of mango can also be given, but again, it is best to offer these cut into small squares in a feeding bowl. If fresh fruits are in short supply, canned items, preferably in

An assortment of fresh fruits and vegetables should be included in your bird's daily diet.

natural juice which can be strained off, should be offered instead. Also, if you find that you can obtain a box of grapes at a cheap price when they are in season, you can deep-freeze these for later use through the year. Simply detach them from their stalks, discarding any grapes which are blemished, and wash them in a colander. Shake off any surplus water and then turn the grapes out onto a clean tray, and place this in the freezer. A day or so later, you can then transfer them into storage bags. The advantage of freezing the grapes in this way is that they will not stick together, so you will be able to remove as many as you

want without any difficulty. Simply leave them to thaw out, or drop them in warm water to speed this process.

Grey Parrots will also enjoy vegetables. Fresh corn-on-the-cob is a particular favorite, and again this can be deep-frozen (after blanching in this case) when in season. It is a valuable source of vitamin A. Carrots also will provide this vitamin, which is only present at low levels in seed, and are usually available throughout the year, even during the winter.

Wash and peel carrots as necessary, and slice them into quarters to make it easier for the parrots to eat. Celery is also accepted by some

Grey Parrots, with stalks again being washed and cut into pieces beforehand.

Green vegetables, and wild plants are often described as "greenfood." These can be cultivated easily if you have a suitable area of land. Spinach beet is very straightforward to grow, irrespective of soil conditions, and the stalks are especially popular with many parrots. It remains green throughout the year, and can even be harvested in the depth of winter.

Other greenfoods are more seasonal. Although it has been traditional for aviculturists to collect wild plants for their birds, many have

All fresh fruits and vegetables should be removed after several hours to prevent the bird from eating spoiled food.

Above: **Darker greens such as broccoli and spinach are higher in their vitamin content than lighter ones such as celery and certain types of lettuce.**

Right: Grey Parrots love to eat apples. It is important to remember to feed all sorts of fresh fruits in moderation only.

contamination from other wild birds, animals, or exhaust fumes from passing automobiles. Always feed green stuff as soon as possible after picking. Likewise, remove any surplus at the end of the day since it could start to turn moldy. It may be worthwhile to dice and chop such items into suitable lengths for your parrot so that there is less waste. Grey Parrots will use their feet to hold such foods. Pieces between 2.5-5cm (1-2in) long are easiest for parrots to handle and eat; larger pieces are usually dropped and birds are reluctant to climb down to the floor

become reluctant to do so during recent years because of fears over the use of herbicides and pollution. Now, however, this option is available, by courtesy of garden seed suppliers. Many of the bird-keeper's favorite items, such as chickweed and dandelions can now be acquired as wild seeds. If planted in a moist corner of the garden they can usually be cropped throughout the summer months.

It is very important to wash all plants collected in the backyard before feeding them to your parrot. This will ensure that there is no trace of

of the aviary to retrieve spilt food.

If you offer such foods at a regular time each day the parrot will soon come to expect this meal. Such items can even be valuable in taming nervous birds, aside from having nutritional benefits. With aviary stock, always provide the food inside the

Grey Parrots have no trouble cracking hard seeds and nuts.

shelter. Here it will remain dry, and is less likely to attract vermin such as mice. Lining the floor of the shelter with newspaper will make it easier to clean up afterwards. It will then be a simple matter of folding up the dirty sheets carefully, and replacing them.

FEEDING METHODS

A special feeding table for the birds to eat from can be built which can directly attach to the shelter. If possible, it should be made to detach easily for cleaning purposes. Grey Parrots are normally reluctant to feed on the floor, certainly until they are used to their surroundings, so a raised table of some kind is usually better at first. When you choose to place the food bowls on the floor in the shelter, be sure to keep them away from overhanging perches, otherwise their contents will be fouled from the droppings of the birds.

The drinking container may be hung somewhere inside the shelter, or it can be hung in a shaded spot of the outside flight. Choose a location close to a perch, so the parrots will have easy access. It is vital to keep an eye on the volume at first, to ensure that it is being used in this location. Birds usually have no problem adapting to a new location of a water container provided it is easily accessible.

During the winter months, it is better to transfer the drinker under cover if possible, where the water will be less likely to freeze. You will need to check the contents regularly on frosty days, to ensure that it does not become frozen.

HOUSEHOLD FOODS

There is a tendency to treat a pet parrot living in the home as a member of the family. Many pet birds are offered a variety of the foods being eaten by the family at the time. Some foods that we eat are not recommended to feed to parrots. Most are safe, when fed in moderation. While fresh nuts are usually quite acceptable (either in their shells or as kernels) never offer salted types, such as peanuts for example. Also, do not be tempted to offer fried or terribly fatty foods. Some Grey Parrots will eat a little cooked meat, even

Opposite Page: **All table treats that are given to a Grey Parrot should be cut into pieces that are easy for the bird to handle.**

chicken, but never offer raw meat, as this could be contaminated with harmful *Salmonella* bacteria.

VITAMIN AND MINERAL SUPPLEMENTS

Both vitamins and minerals are present, to some extent, in a basic diet designed for parrots. Supplementation is often advisable, especially during the molting and breeding periods. Seeds are low in calcium, which is vital for a healthy bone structure and for the formation of egg-shells during the breeding season. This mineral is normally supplied in the form of cuttlefish bone, which can be purchased from your local pet store.

The bone should be attached to the side of the bird's cage, close to a perch. The soft side must face the bird so that it can easily nibble it away. Special clips of various designs can be purchased from your local pet store especially for this purpose. Cuttlefish bone should always be available throughout the year. Just before the start of the breeding period, parrots are likely to consume more cuttlefish, as the hen prepares to lay her eggs.

In addition to cuttlefish bone, you can offer an iodine block to your parrots. These pinkish blocks are also

Vitamin and mineral supplements are an important part of every bird's diet. They are available in a variety of forms that can be purchased at pet shops everywhere. Photo courtesy of Hagen Products.

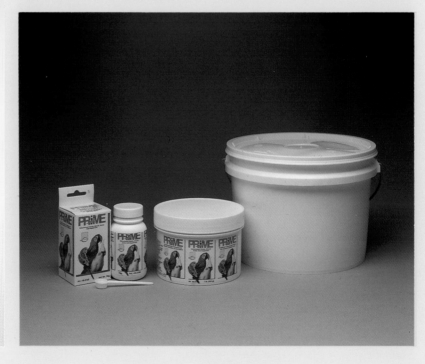

available from your pet store. They can simply be hung in place near a perch by twisting the wire tags set in the block around the mesh of the parrot's quarters. Iodine is used by the thyroid gland to manufacture hormones. These stimulate the level of the parrot's activity, and help to encourage breeding behavior.

You can also obtain a variety of general vitamin and mineral supplements in powder form from your pet store. Some brands also contain amino acids such as lysine which may be deficient in a parrot's diet, and so are preferable as a result. Each variety will have instructions telling you how often it should be given to the parrot and in what quantity.

Do not be tempted to give more than the recommended dosage because this could be harmful over a period of time. Although you can sprinkle the powder over dried seed, this is fairly wasteful. Only a small amount will actually stick to the seed, of which the outer husks are discarded anyway. Instead, shake the required amount lightly over fruit, greenfood, or even soaked seed. The powder will stick much better to these moist surfaces, and more will actually be consumed.

Normally, there is no

The nails of some Grey Parrots can become so long that they will actually get in the way when the bird attempts to eat with its foot! You may either clip the nails yourself, or take the bird to an avian veterinarian.

Continue to offer your pet Grey different food items even if it does not seem interested. A bird's taste changes over time, and what was once disliked soon becomes a favorite food!

Grey Parrots can be rewarded for their performance with small, favored treats.

difficulty in persuading parrots to take supplements in this form. These tend to be more comprehensive than those available in fluid form. The liquid type can be distributed in the drinking water. Be sure to wash out the drinker thoroughly when using products of this type. Always discard treated water within twenty-four hours to ensure freshness. Such products should always be kept in the dark,

otherwise their potency may be affected. They are most useful in situations where Grey Parrots are reluctant to take foods to which powdered supplements adhere well.

When choosing products of this type in your pet store, be sure to select one intended specifically for birds. Those produced for other animals can be less satisfactory, containing vitamin D_2 for example, rather than vitamin D_3 which is the form required by birds. If in doubt, do not hesitate to ask for advice. Providing your parrots with a varied and balanced diet will help to ensure that they enjoy a long, active life. Good feeding also plays a critical role in achieving breeding success.

BREEDING AFRICAN GREY PARROTS

The first vital aspect of breeding African Grey Parrots is to ensure that the birds which you have are in fact a true pair. Various suggestions have been made about how you can separate cocks and hens. Cocks may have broader heads than hens, and the area of bare skin around their eyes may be more pointed rather than rounded in shape. These features are not consistent, however, they may prove a means of distinguishing the individuals of a pair.

Since they occur over such a wide area of Africa, there is bound to be a natural variation in the size of these birds, therefore, the size of a bird is not a reliable sexual distinction. Somewhat more significant, however, is the depth of coloration over the wings of adult

At about two weeks old, young Grey Parrots have begun to lose most of their white down, and gray down begins to appear.

birds. In the case of cocks, where more melanin is deposited at maturity, this area of the body is darker, as compared to the hens. This can be a helpful guide if you are considering a number of birds, and trying to pick a pair.

The most reliable method now in use to recognize pairs of Grey Parrots is surgical sexing. Many dealers now offer birds which have been sexed in this way, with the

At six weeks old this Grey Parrot has already done a lot of growing. Baby parrots grow very fast. In another six weeks this baby will have almost attained adult size, and will be completely feathered.

initials "S.S." displayed against the price. The technique, undertaken by veterinarians, entails the administration of an anesthetic in the first instance. A small cut is made on the parrot's left flank, between the last ribs, which is just large enough to allow the insertion of a viewing instrument, usually an endoscope, into the body cavity. Then, by looking through this equipment, it is possible to see the parrot's internal reproductive organs. The presence of an ovary denotes a hen, while a testis confirms that the bird is a cock. Afterwards, the parrot should recover uneventfully from the procedure within a short time. The wound does not normally require any stitching or other attention, but be sure to follow any recommendations made by the veterinarian.

An increasing number of veterinarians are now involved in exotic avian medicine, and able to undertake surgical sexing. This is a very safe procedure, in spite of the use of an anesthetic. Only very fit birds should be exposed to this type of procedure. Therefore, if you are taking any birds for surgical sexing, be sure to alert your veterinarian beforehand if you suspect anything could be amiss. Very obese birds also present a risk to anesthetic than those of normal weight. The cost of surgical sexing is relatively inexpensive, and because the method entails direct viewing of the sex organs, it is usually quite reliable. Occasionally, mistakes do occur, especially if the birds were sexed by this means at a young age. The veterinarian will also be able to tell you whether the bird in question is soon likely to breed, having seen the state of the ovary for example. Diseases of which you may be unaware, affecting internal body organs such as the liver, may also be detected during an examination of this kind.

There are other methods of significance for sexing parrots which are being used these days. Therefore if you are seeking to pair up any type of parrot, talk to your avian vet about what method would be best for the birds you keep.

Chromosomal karyotyping is another method which is being used more often these days. It requires only a small drop of blood from a

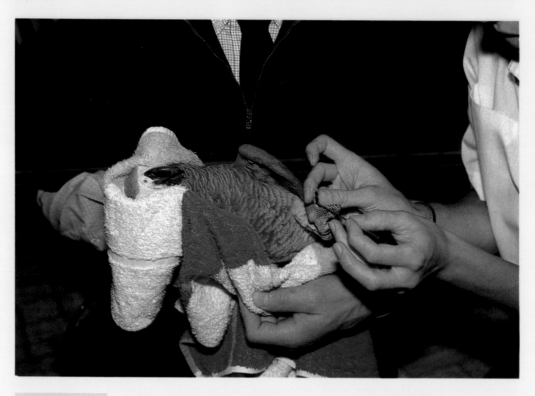

A blood sample can easily be obtained by clipping into the quick of a claw while the bird is restrained by hand in a towel.

feather to perform a test. It relies on the fact that all characteristics of the bird, including its gender, are determined by genes located on chromosomes. By creating a chromosomal map or karyotype, it is then possible to locate the pair of sex chromosomes. They have a distinctive appearance, since those of hens are of uneven length, compared with the situation in cock birds.

COMPATIBILITY

Even if you are certain you have a true pair of Grey Parrots, there is another factor which will be highly significant for breeding success. This is the compatibility of the individual birds themselves. It is for this reason that the most satisfactory way of breeding these parrots is still to house a number together, even if they have already been sexed, and allow them to choose their own partners.

Compatible pairs will show clear signs of pair-bonding. They will remain in close proximity to each other, and feed and preen together. This area of parrot breeding is not well studied at present, but certainly, if you have a breeding pair, it is inadvisable to split up the birds and give them new partners. They appear to pair for life under normal circumstances. You should be able to detect signs of pair-bonding by careful observation.

It will actually be worth spending time watching the birds that are on offer prior to the purchase. Some birds do take to each other readily, however, there are those that will simply not get along. Sometimes if a pair does not seem to take to each other, a temporary separation, and then reintroduction improves the situation. Failing this, your only option will be to seek new partners for this particular pair. You may be able to arrange an exchange with a fellow aviculturist in a similar situation.

It has only been during the last few years, with the advent of large scale captive-breeding units, that the significance of compatibility in pairs of Grey Parrots has been appreciated to any extent. Kept under identical conditions and fed in exactly the same manner, it has been noted that some pairs settle down together, breeding readily and regularly, whereas others refuse to breed at all. Often, a change of partners has overcome the problem.

Grey Parrots often become protective of their young. If this youngster is to be taken away from his parents for hand-rearing, it may be difficult to get him out without the parents attacking.

NEST BOXES

A nest box for a pair of Grey Parrots must be sturdy enough to withstand their powerful beaks. For this reason, bird keepers have designed boxes from all sorts of materials, such as a metal trash can.

It is a good idea to have a nest box in place in the parrots' quarters right from the outset, even before you introduce them here. Adding a box later can cause a disturbance, which will upset the birds and may actually distract them from breeding.

The nest box needs to be made out of stout timber, at least 2.5cm (1in) in thickness, partly to deter the parrots' beaks, and also to insulate the interior. Greys have bred in nest boxes of various designs.

They often prefer a reasonably deep box, measuring perhaps 60cm (2ft) from top to bottom, with an entrance hole about 10cm (4in) in diameter cut at the front, just below the roof.

The internal area of the box should be about 25cm (10in) square. A perch positioned several inches below the entrance hole is also recommended, so the parrots can have easy access to their nest site. Inside, running down from the base of the entrance hole to the floor, there should be a mesh ladder, so that the parrots can move in and out of the box easily.

The ladder must be held in place very firmly, with netting staples running down each side. Otherwise, if it becomes dislodged, it will block off the bottom of the box, where there may be eggs and chicks. You must also ensure that there are no rough edges on the sides of the mesh, which could injure a parrot. Trim the cut strands back as close as possible to the neighboring vertical strand, and then rub the edges down with a metal file as an additional precaution.

You may be able to buy a suitable nest box from your pet store, especially during the spring months, although it is not too difficult to make one if necessary. Having cut and prepared the various component parts, screw them together. It will then be easier to dismantle the box for cleaning and repair. Always check that you have easy access to the interior of the box. This is an important aspect because you may, at some time, have to remove eggs or young chicks from the box. Although it is useful to have a hinged roof, this becomes less valuable

Hand-feeding baby Grey Parrots is a very dedicated and time-consuming job.

Young Grey Parrots do not leave the nest until they are about ten weeks old. The adult male often takes over the feeding duties after the chicks leave the nest and until they are weaned.

once the nest box is actually positioned in the aviary. It will then be difficult to both reach down inside, and see what you are doing in the box at the same time. A side-hatch is an invaluable option. The bottom of the hatch should be at least 10cm (4in) above the floor of the nest box, so that chicks and eggs cannot fall out when it is opened.

Fix the hatch with hinges so that it opens outwards and upwards. You can also add a hook, with a catch at the appropriate position above. You can then hold the hatch open, and have both hands free at the same

time. Similarly, it is a good idea to be able to close the hatch in position with a small bolt, ensuring that it is a secure fit. Otherwise, the parrots are likely to gnaw at this access point around its edges. Should the interior of the nest box become too bright, they may choose to abandon it.

Positioning
Grey Parrots prefer to nest off the ground. It is common to position the nest box close to the roof of the aviary. Choose a suitable location, under cover. This can be in the outside flight, provided that there is no risk of the interior of the nest box

becoming flooded.

Place several nest boxes in different locations to give the birds a choice of nesting sites. One can be located in a dark corner and another in the shelter of their aviary where more seclusion may be available. You must ensure that the weight of the nest box is properly supported, otherwise not only may the box fall down with catastrophic results, but the structure of the aviary itself may also be damaged as a result.

Brackets provide the easiest means of attachment. Check that no screws protrude into the nest box, especially through the floor where they could cause breakage of eggs. Depending on the arrangement of timber in the frames, you may be able to attach "L" shaped brackets on each side and below the nest box for added security. The entrance hole to the nest box should be located in the front, so the parrots have easy access.

A suitable lining material is important for the floor of the nest box. Although peat has been popular in the past for this purpose, it dries out readily and becomes dusty. Up-turned grass turfs can also be

hazardous and may contain sharp stones which could damage the eggs. Certainly without doubt, the best option is to allow the Greys to make their own nest litter, by providing small blocks of a suitable softwood, cut into lengths each measuring about 5cm (2in). Prior to the onset of the laying period, the parrots will start to "work" their nest box. They will chew up the lining to form a bed on which the eggs will be laid. Keep a close eye on the situation. If necessary, add further strips of wood for the parrots to whittle away.

Avoid offering contaminated wood, such as rotten branches because these will introduce fungal spores and other harmful micro-organisms to the nest site. A high level of contamination in the nest litter inevitably leads to a decrease in hatchability. An added advantage here is that by offering wood for the parrots to gnaw, their attention is distracted away from attacking the actual timber used to make the nest box.

BREEDING INDOORS

Commercial breeders tend to opt for breeding

their birds in cages, and so with less space available, they often prefer to hang nest boxes outside the cages. This will make inspection easier than if the box were located within the cage. Again, brackets provide the easiest means of support, although you will now need to cut a hole carefully in the cage mesh so the parrots can move in and out through the entrance hole. If you only cut out just sufficient for this purpose, the remainder of the front of the box will remain out of the birds' reach. In addition, you

can convert the cage back for stock housing rather than breeding purposes at a later date simply by patching the hole carefully with another piece of mesh. It is important that there are no loose ends of sharp mesh protruding in this vicinity, as these could injure the birds.

With indoor housing, Grey Parrots can be encouraged to breed over a longer period than if they are kept in an outdoor aviary. It also appears possible, at least to some extent, to condition the birds so that they start breeding at the same time. This can obviously be advantageous if you are planning to raise the chicks by hand, since you will have the offspring of a number of pairs all at a similar stage.

Artificial lighting and heating are an integral part of an indoor breeding set-up. Fluorescent tubes, which emit light similar to that of natural sunlight, are usually recommended. This is because they include light from the ultra-violet end of the spectrum, which, when falling on the parrots' plumage, enables them to synthesize vitamin D_3 in a natural way. This chemical is especially vital during the breeding season, to ensure that adequate calcium is available in the blood stream for healthy eggshells. Heating will help to prevent eggs laid during the colder part of the year from becoming chilled, by raising the environmental temperature. A reading about 13°C (55°F) is adequate in most cases. Commercial breeding of Grey Parrots is likely to take a number of years before becoming successful, as the birds will inevitably take time to settle in their quarters.

A metal band on a bird's leg can be one of two types. Closed, coded metal bands prove that a bird was domestic-bred, while a split metal band denotes a bird that was legally quarantined after import.

EGG-LAYING

The behavior of Grey Parrots alters as they come into breeding condition. Some become more noisy, and tame birds may show signs of aggression towards their owners. Prior to feeding his mate, a cock bird will make a number of vertical movements of his head and neck. Such gestures become more common as mating approaches, and sometimes, he may lower his wings to display the more colorful red markings of the tail area to his mate. The eyes themselves become more yellowish during periods of sexual excitement as the irises become constricted for short periods. When she is finally ready to mate, the hen will lower herself on the perch, and invite the male to mate her. Only one mating is necessary to fertilize a clutch of eggs.

In conjunction with their courtship behavior, the parrots will spend increasingly longer periods of time in their nest box. At first, they are likely to be nervous, and will come out readily at the slightest sound. Gradually, however, if the birds are left alone, they will settle down and start preparing the nesting site in earnest. The male will join his mate inside for periods, although he does not take any part in the incubation process once the eggs have been laid.

When the hen emerges from the nest box, you may be able to see a slight swelling above the vent, which will often be apparent just before she starts laying. This is quite normal. Similarly, her droppings may also change in consistency at this stage, and have a very pungent odor.

Unless you decide to check the nest box, you may not be aware of when the hen first lays. This is because she is unlikely to start incubating at this stage. Only when the second or third egg is laid will she begin sitting in earnest. Grey Parrots normally produce clutches of two or three eggs, although four is not unknown. These are usually laid with an interval of two and sometimes three days between them.

The hen ensures that her chicks will be of a more even size, and hatch close together by waiting to begin incubating her clutch until it is complete. The average incubation period lasts between 28 and 30 days, although it may be slightly longer before the first egg hatches, depending on when the hen began sitting.

Newly-hatched Grey Parrots are covered in thick white down, which contrasts with their black toenails. Do not worry when you see that the lower mandible of the chick appears longer than the upper—this is quite normal. Emerging from an egg weighing 19-22g (0.6-0.8oz), a young Grey Parrot will be about 14g (0.5oz) on hatching. Within two weeks, most of the white down is lost, and replaced by the early signs of the developing gray down feathers. These appear as dark dots on the skin. The tongue, which is pink at first, gradually changes to black over the course of three or four weeks. By five weeks old, the chicks are covered in light gray down, and there are clear signs of their wing feathers becoming apparent. Their distinctive red tail feathers should be

Grey Parrot eggs compared to a chicken egg. Upon hatching, a Grey Parrot will weigh approximately 14g (0.5oz). Their growth rate is rapid, and at the time of fledging can weigh 336g (12oz).

Grey Parrots will remove the bark from tree branches and use it as nesting materials.

evident about a week later. Traces of gray will remain visible at the tip of the tail of young Grey Parrots, until they molt for the first time at a year old. By ten weeks old, the chicks will virtually be fully feathered, and soon afterwards, they will leave the nest site for the first time. It will be several more weeks before they can feed themselves independently.

After the chicks have fledged, however, the male assumes greater responsibility for them, whereas the hen may start making preparations for another clutch of eggs. By the time they leave the nest, the young Grey Parrots will weigh about 336g (12oz)—a significant increase from their hatching weight. They should be moved to separate quarters once they are feeding independently.

THE REARING PERIOD

It is probably best to leave the parrots alone through the incubation period, provided that there is no obvious cause for concern. Right at the start of the laying period, there is a slight risk that the hen could become egg-bound, but this is far from common, especially if she has been receiving a good diet. The signs and treatment of egg-binding will be described later.

Keeping a close watch on the parrots' food consumption is one of the best indicators of when the chicks have hatched. You may also hear the young parrots calling for their food, especially in the evening, just before dusk. At this stage, it is vital to offer as wide a range of foods as possible. Soaked seed is easier to digest than dry seed, and even if the adult birds have refused green stuff and other items previously, they may now accept such foods avidly, when there are chicks in the nest.

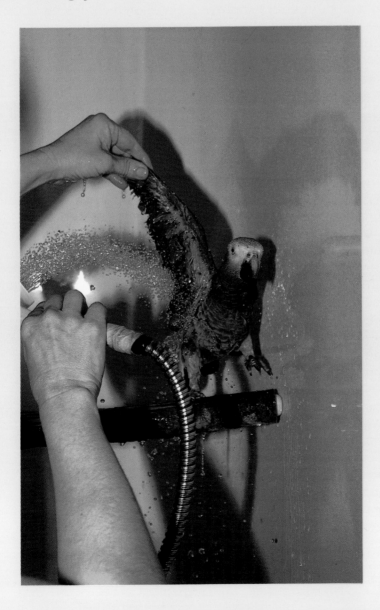

Many Grey Parrots enjoy showers. Showers and baths keep the bird's overall plumage in healthy condition.

Their water consumption will also rise noticeably, especially during hot weather. It may be worthwhile to provide an additional drinker, so the birds do not run short of fluid. This applies particularly if they are eating pellets, which, because of their dry nature, tend to raise the parrots' normal fluid intake in any event.

It is probably fair to state that most losses of chicks occur during the first week or so, possibly because the adults have not been offered a suitably varied diet. In addition, young Greys nesting for the first time may prove to be poor parents, and neglect their chicks.

If you suspect that something is amiss during this time, you will need to attract the adults out of the nest box. This will allow you to inspect the interior without difficulty. If the pair remains inside while you attempt to do this, they are likely either to lunge at your hand, or attempt to fly out, harming eggs and chicks in the process. The provision of their favorite food, or a gentle tap on the side of the nest box should be enough to persuade them to come out into the aviary.

Contented, well-fed chicks rarely make much noise. In contrast, those which are short of food call far more persistently. It is easy to tell whether or not a chick is hungry by looking at the state of its crop, located at the base of the neck. In a chick which has been recently fed, the crop appears quite swollen, protruding from the body. Poorly-fed chicks have empty crops for long periods, and apart from crying, soon appear weak. This may call for you to intervene and feed the young by hand. This task is now carried out routinely in some collections, as a means of maximizing on the reproductive potential of the parrots. By removing either the eggs, or even chicks within a day or so of hatching, it is possible to encourage the adult birds to nest again within a short

Sometimes a bird's band may appear to bother its leg. This is not impossible, however, it is fairly uncommon. If you believe it to be a problem, consult your avian vet immediately.

period of time. One pair of Grey Parrots, kept by Mrs. Velma Hart of Long Beach, California, produced 87 chicks in the period 1962 to 1974, as a result of their young being raised by hand.

It is now quite straight forward to raise Grey Parrot chicks by hand, but it is a very time-consuming task. Regular feedings, every two hours or so, are necessary at first. It will of course be nearly three months before the chicks are independent, so if you are not in a position to meet these needs, do not attempt this unless it is absolutely necessary. There are now some aviculturists who offer both incubation and hand-raising services.

It is worthwhile to make inquiries in your area (even before your parrots start nesting) as to what facilities of this type are available to you. Your pet store, or the advertisement columns of bird-keeping magazines, are likely to be useful starting points.

If you decide to attempt hand-raising chicks yourself, you will need a brooder where they can be kept warm. Some firms offer brooders, although if necessary, it is not difficult to build a suitable cabinet. You will need an

The powder down feathers of a Grey Parrot create a fine white dust that certain people are allergic to. As the parrot shakes off, this powder can be seen. Plenty of baths help to keep this dust to a minimum.

adjustable, reliable heat source, ventilation holes, a thermometer to monitor the temperature within, and an access door.

Some breeders have even converted a fishtank into brooding quarters for their parrot chicks. The chicks will need to be maintained at a temperature of about 37.2°C (99°F) when they first hatch. It will then be possible to lower this gradually.

The chicks themselves should be restrained in a suitable receptacle, such as a clean, empty ice-cream container. Paper towelling is preferable as bedding for them; it is easy to change at each feed, and will not be harmful. A complete rearing food can be obtained from your local pet store. Several are now

Breeding records are very ○ important to keep. Knowing such things as incubation time, clutch number, and chick's weight, help you to know when things might be amiss with future breedings.

available as a result of considerable intensive research over the past few years. They have removed the need for trial-and-error mixtures, offering instead a consistently balanced diet. Avoid suddenly changing brands during the rearing period because this can cause a serious upset in the chicks' digestive system, unless the substitution is made very gradually.

Complete rearing foods are easy to prepare, and only need to be mixed with water. Take care to ensure that they are neither too hot, which can burn the chick's mouth, or too cold as this is likely to chill baby parrots. Always follow the instructions as directed on the packaging.

Although some aviculturists prefer to use

a syringe for hand-raising parrots it is usually better to opt for a teaspoon. This is easier to use and allows the chicks to feed naturally at their own speed. The constant trauma caused by a syringe with a tube attached can prove fatal to young chicks. With a teaspoon, you simply need to bend the edges inwards, to create a channel through which the food will flow directly into the chick's mouth.

The surrounding in which you feed the chicks must be warm so they do not become chilled when they are out of the brooder. The area also ought to be well-lit, and at a convenient height for you. A table with a desk-light attached is useful in this regard. Never try to rush feeding, especially at first, however, allow the chicks to feed at their own pace.

You can monitor their progress by watching their crops fill with food, and the young parrots will soon indicate when they have eaten sufficiently. After a feed, be sure to wipe carefully around the beak, to remove any deposits of food, before these harden. If this is not done they can cause

In the wild, a Grey Parrot becomes camouflaged when perched in a tree. Because of this, the Greys will eat and sleep here.

It is easy to tell when a chick needs to be fed. The crop will empty out and a chick will beg incessantly.

malformation of the beak over a period of time. Also try to prevent food dribbling down onto the plumage, as this will be unsightly, and can be difficult to remove successfully. Soiling of the plumage may also encourage feather-plucking.

It is a good idea to weigh the chicks every day, so that you can note their development. Problems can often be revealed initially by a loss of weight, although this is normal in the period immediately before fledging.

One of the most common rearing problems that you are likely to encounter is a chick whose crop fails to empty properly. It may simply be that it is cold. Check the brooder temperature in the first instance. If this appears normal, then a dilute solution of molasses and water given by tube into the crop may prove an effective remedy.

An occasional problem, which is sometimes encountered in Grey Parrot chicks, is swollen toes. This problem usually becomes apparent once the youngsters are quite

well-feathered. Although an infection could be the cause, especially if the feet have been allowed to become dirty through the hand-rearing phase, it seems more likely to be a nutritional problem, associated with the hand-raising food.

The tip of one or more toes, including the area around the nail, becomes progressively swollen, while at the neighboring joint above, there is a clear shrinkage of tissue. Ultimately with this form of dry gangrene, the affected part of the toe sloughs off several weeks later, with little if any associated bleeding. The parrot is otherwise unaffected, and can lead a normal life. The cause of the condition is unclear—it seems likely that a vitamin B deficiency in the rearing mixture may be implicated. This again shows the importance of using a standardized reputable formula for the purpose.

As the chicks grow, they will need larger quarters. Low perches can be added to their enclosure, and soaked sunflower seed, which proves a useful weaning food, can be introduced to their diet. Do not be in a hurry to complete the weaning process, since this can be harmful.

BREEDING RECORDS

Grey Parrots were first bred successfully outside of Africa in France, during the 1770s, when a pair nested successfully over several years. Since then, they have been bred repeatedly. The first British success was achieved in 1843, with a pair which had been kept as household pets. A flannel nest was provided for the hen, near an open fire to keep her warm. Here she managed to rear a single chick.

One of the earliest American records is equally bizarre. The breeder in question, Gilbert Lee, described how in 1903 he started a breeding program with these parrots. He released seventeen into a cow barn, feeding and watering them entirely from outside the building.

When he inspected the colony three years later, Lee claimed to have discovered there were a further sixty-seven parrots present, with eleven skeletons on the floor. Stung by the skepticism which followed his statement, Lee began breeding Greys again in 1930, on more conventional lines. He was first successful in 1934,

Certain household plants are dangerous for birds to nibble on. To be safe, keep all plants away from your pet.

and obtained consistent results thereafter.

Certainly, once you have a pair of Greys which breed successfully, you should expect them to continue nesting every year for well over a decade. Although the cost of these parrots has risen quite considerably during recent years, it should be possible to recoup some of your outlay by the sale of the odd youngster from time to time. Now, it is also important to plan for the future, so why not try to find another breeder who will join with you in breeding Greys over several generations?

By swapping youngsters, you will be well on the way to setting up new pairs. Young birds housed together from an early age are also more likely to develop a strong pair bond after maturity than adult birds introduced to each other for the first time at this stage. Although chicks may not breed until they are four years old, imported Greys can also take long to settle in their quarters, and their age will be unknown.

AFRICAN GREY PARROTS AS PETS

The powers of mimicry of the Grey Parrot are almost legendary. They are without doubt the most talented birds when it comes to reproducing the sound of the human voice, and amassing a vocabulary of words and phrases. Presently unchallenged as the top talker on record is "Prudle," who was obtained as a baby in Uganda during 1958. He won the "Best talking parrot-like bird" class, held in England as part of the National Exhibition of Cage and Aviary Birds for twelve years in succession. Prudle's vocabulary is estimated to consist of over 800 words, and he can repeat sentences containing twenty-one separate words, in the correct order.

Unfortunately, however, not all Grey Parrots learn to mimic as well as Prudle. You need to start with a recently-fledged youngster, and have considerable patience as a teacher. It seems likely that some parrots are simply more talented as mimics than

By placing your hand directly in front of the Grey Parrot, it will have no other choice but to step up onto this. If the bird seems reluctant, you may press your hand gently against its breast to force the issue.

It is often comical to watch a pet Grey play with its favored toy. They really can get into an uproar if their toy begins to act up!

others, but it is also important not to rush the teaching process, otherwise you are likely to confuse your new companion.

TALKING TECHNIQUES

Start by repeating the name you have chosen for your pet. Every time you enter the room, say "Hello Prudle," for example. It is important to capture the parrot's attention for training purposes. Similarly, when you first draw the curtains or blinds in the morning, you can repeat "Good morning Prudle." The activity, combined with your presence, should help the parrot to learn these simple phrases quite rapidly.

When you are teaching your pet, try to avoid obvious distractions in the room, such as the presence of a dog, as this is likely to upset your bird's power of concentration. Grey Parrots, although talented mimics, are often shy, and so may refuse to respond if their routine is disturbed. For this reason, they are not always good at performing in front of strangers.

Greys will also learn to whistle simple tunes quite easily, probably because whistling is similar to the sounds of their natural call notes. You can use either pre-recorded cassette tapes or records to reinforce the teaching periods. Indeed, if you have to leave your parrot alone for much of the day, it will appreciate the companionship provided by your voice on tape or a radio. Commercial training records are also successful, so if you do not wish to make a tape you can purchase this from your local pet store.

As you expand the parrot's vocabulary, be sure to repeat the early words which it has already learned, in correct sequence. Otherwise there is a risk that the bird may become muddled, and begin to jumble words and phrases. If you have acquired a Grey Parrot which is already talking, it may be shy at first, so do not assume that you have been deceived by descriptions of the bird's talking ability. Within a week or so, it should have settled sufficiently to run through its repertoire properly.

The problem may then arise that the bird has learned undesirable words or sounds, such as the ringing of the telephone which can be very confusing. Unfortunately, there is no simple solution to difficulties of this nature. Obviously, you will not repeat the offending word, or you may move the parrot so that hopefully it will not hear the disturbing sound.

The only other option is to cover the cage with a heavy cloth whenever the parrot utters the word or sound. By learning to associate these sounds with the onset of sudden darkness for five minutes or so, the parrot can be deterred from transgressing again over a period of time. This may prove a slow process, and can extend over the course of several months. Teaching new words or sounds can also help, since then the results of the earlier lessons may be forgotten.

TAMING

Part of the pleasure of keeping a pet parrot, especially a Grey, is the companionship which can

Be sure your pet Grey has had plenty of time to stretch before you place it back inside of its cage.

A Grey Parrot is a lifelong commitment. Barring any illness or accidents, it may live in excess of fifty years.

result from having a tame bird, aside from its powers of mimicry. If you start with a hand-raised youngster, you can be certain that it will already be tame and relatively fearless. It is then a matter of encouraging these traits, before you let the parrot out into the room. You will need to be able to pick the bird up easily within the home, rather than having it flying around freely, and proving almost impossible to catch.

The first step is to persuade the parrot to perch on your hand in the cage. This can be accomplished quite easily by positioning your hand horizontally against the perch, and then gradually moving it over the top, touching the parrot's toes as necessary.

It is vital to move slowly and deliberately at all times, so as not to frighten the bird. By gently prying the parrot's toes off the perch with your outstretched hand, the likelihood is that the bird will then transfer its grip to your fingers.

Once you have accomplished this stage, be certain to give the parrot a reward, such as a piece of fruit. Repeat the technique until the bird has no hesitation in perching on your hand. You can then gradually withdraw your hand from the cage, encouraging the bird to follow you through the opening. This part is more tricky, especially if the door is relatively small.

If necessary, you may be able to entice your pet to come out by offering a favorite tidbit of fruit. Always try to encourage the parrot to take such items by hand, even through the sides of the cage, as again, this will reinforce the bond between bird and owner. Only if such items are refused after five minutes or so should you leave them, to see if the parrot will eat them by itself.

Once the parrot leaves its cage readily and perches on your arm, you have a tame pet. Greys then often like to climb up onto your shoulder where they may start pulling your hair or nibbling at your ear. This is rarely done with malice, but appears to be similar to the preening behavior of a pair of birds. The back of the neck is a favored site for this show of affection, and it is surprising how gentle Grey Parrots can be, in spite of their fearsome beaks.

SAFETY PRECAUTIONS
Several basic precautions must be taken before you contemplate letting your parrot out of its cage. All windows in a room should be closed, and cats and dogs should have no access to the room where the parrot will be. Fish tanks should either be removed or covered, while open fires of any type must be suitably screened, so there is no risk of the parrot burning itself.

Even a very tame bird should never be left unsupervised in a room. Aside from the damage that it could inflict with its sharp beak, there is also a possibility that the parrot could chew through a live electric cable, with fatal consequences. A number of house plants are potentially poisonous to birds, such as Dumb Cane

Common household items, such as this padlock, prove to be fun and exciting toys for Grey Parrots. Other fun things are empty paper towel rolls, and a key ring with several spare keys included.

A ball point pen is another household item that is a favored toy by Grey Parrots. It would be a good idea, however, to remove the ink so that a messy accident does not occur.

(*Dieffenbachia picta*), and should either be removed from the room or the parrot supervised in such a way that it cannot eat any of the foliage.

Lead paintwork in older properties presents a similar hazard, as does pipework, although through the water supply rather than directly. Grey Parrots appear quite susceptible to the toxic effects of lead. Loss of co-ordination is a typical symptom. Filtered or still, bottled water may be better if you have old pipework in your home.

WING CLIPPING

In order to preserve the bird's mobility, but at the same time protect it from danger, you may decide to clip the flight feathers across one wing. If you are in any doubt about the procedure, ask your veterinarian for advice. Wing-clipping is not permanent, unlike the operation known as pinioning. The cut feathers will be replaced at the next molt. You will need a sharp pair of scissors, and someone who can hold the parrot's wing open for you. Then, leaving the outermost flight feather intact, cut across the remainder, low down just above where the shaft broadens out into the vane of the feather. If you trim the feathers at a lower point, there is a risk that bleeding might occur, especially just after a molt. At this stage, the feathers may still be receiving an extensive blood supply through the shaft.

Carried out properly, wing-clipping should not cause a parrot any harm, although you might find that the bird may be rather subdued after being handled for this purpose.

STAND TRAINING

Once out of their quarters, many parrots like to perch on top of their cage, and will go back inside to feed when they want. It is a good idea to encourage this behavior because it lessens the risk of droppings being deposited on furniture around the room. You may be able to find a suitable wooden perch which clips on above the roof of the cage at your local pet

Grey Parrots will often "check" how sturdy an item is before they will step up onto it by sampling it with their beak. Do not be frightened and pull away because it will cause the bird to clamp on harder, and may even inflict a nasty bite.

Play stands provide fun and excitement for your pet while it is away from its cage.

store. If not, you can make one yourself, which will be quite straightforward.

You will need a suitable length of wooden dowelling (to run along the top of the cage) plus thick strands of wire which will be used to hold it in place. Twist and secure the wire tightly at either end of the roof of the cage. Then fix it to hold the length of dowelling by folding it around each end, keeping the wire tightly coiled here. It is then simply a matter of fixing the loose ends back on the roof of the cage, on the opposite side from the first point of attachment.

Aim to create a triangular arrangement, with the perch itself forming the upper pinnacle when looked at from each end. The strands of wire form the upper sloping sides when tied on the roof of the cage. This is then in effect the horizontal side of the triangle.

You may also be able to obtain a separate perch stand for your parrot, as distinct from one which fits onto the cage. Such units are "T" shaped with a circular or rectangular tray beneath to catch droppings, seed husks, and spilt food.

Your parrot will soon learn to use the stand, and should be quite happy perching here. If necessary, with a "T" shaped stand, encourage the parrot to perch on your hand once it is out of its cage, and simply transfer it directly across to the new stand. Grey Parrots, with their intelligent natures, will soon learn to perch here, especially if they have food and water pots available at each end.

A CLOSE RELATIONSHIP

Allowing the parrot out into the room on a regular basis will enable you to have a much closer rapport with your pet. Here, it should feed readily from your hand, and even encourage you to show your affection, by tickling it at the back of the neck. This is the area where members of a pair will preen each other. A Grey Parrot will often indicate a desire to be scratched here by its owner. It will tilt its head slightly on one side,

making the neck region more accessible.

It is a good idea to approach initially from the side rather than directly past the beak, just in case your parrot becomes shy at the last moment. This then gives less of a risk of being bitten, as the bird can move to the other side to escape your attentions if it so wishes. Once your parrot signals its approval, however, you are well on the way to establishing a close bond.

Nevertheless, do encourage all members of the family to become involved. Unfortunately, Grey Parrots can easily develop into "one person birds," and may actually be hostile to other people in the household. This may not appear to cause

Most Grey Parrots enjoy perching on their owner's hand or arm. These are sturdy places for the Grey to stand and feel secure.

A Grey Parrot may be frightened of new toys at first. It may be a good idea to accustom your pet to a new object outside of its cage before it becomes a permanent part of the cage.

any difficulty in the short-term, but problems can arise if you are then away from home for any length of time. Apart from showing its aggression towards other people, perhaps by biting them as they clean out the cage, the bird may start pining for you to the extent that it begins to pluck its feathers. This, apart from being unsightly, can be very difficult to combat successfully.

BATHING

Birds that have never received a regular bath or spray will have to be accustomed to bathing times. Kept outdoors, Greys will bathe in a

shower of rain which helps to keep their plumage in good condition. Inside, deprived of water for bathing, their feathering tends to become dry and brittle, losing its normally sleek appearance. Perhaps partly because of its frustration at not being able to keep its feathers in position, the parrot then starts to pull them out.

It is therefore important that you spray your parrot once or twice every week. Start by removing the seed pot. A good time to spray is just before you clean the cage out so that the damp paper on the floor will be removed immediately. Use a plant sprayer with a fine jet, and fill this with tepid water. You can add a plumage conditioner—several different brands are available from pet stores. At first, your parrot may be rather scared, so always point the nozzle in an upward direction above the cage. The droplets of water will then fall down gently on the parrot, rather than squirting out at it directly. There is no need to soak the bird's plumage—if you do, it may develop a chill.

Never be tempted to place the parrot in front of a window to dry off. Even on a moderately sunny day, unable to escape from

Grey Parrots usually do not like to be approached from the front —this motion frightens them. It is better to bring your finger directly to the bird's lower mandible, scratch under the chin, and work your way around to the back of the bird's neck.

the sun, your parrot could die of heat-stroke.

PET PARROTS OUTDOORS

If at any stage you decide to take your parrot outside on a warm day, avoid placing the cage in direct sunshine. Although Grey Parrots originate from tropical areas, they can always find cover. Also avoid the sun when its rays are at their hottest. They prefer instead to be active in the early morning and late afternoon, when the heat is less intense.

You must never leave your parrot alone when it is outside. It is otherwise likely to attract the neighborhood cats. Also, be sure that all door fastenings are secure. Remember that even a very tame parrot may fly off if it is frightened. Outdoors, in a strange environment, there is a considerable risk that

The life of some Grey Parrots may seem as if it is all play, however, to the bird it must seem like hard work! This Grey parrot seems determined to get the leather key chain off of the keys.

your Grey Parrot would disappear, so do not open the cage door here. Should you lose your bird at any stage however, contact local radio stations, who may operate a "lost and found" pets notice board on air.

Pet stores in your area should also be alerted, as well as the police, veterinarians, and animal welfare groups, any of whom may be approached by someone who sees or finds the parrot. As an additional precaution in case their parrot escapes, some owners teach their birds to repeat either their address, or a telephone number.

Having located the bird, you may be able to tempt it down to you by offering a favorite item of food, and calling to your pet. Alternatively, you may have to resort to trying to trap it, using its cage. Place this in a prominent position, such as on top of a shed roof for example, checking that the food and water pots are full.

Attach a suitable length of string to the door of the cage, and then wait. Hopefully, the parrot will fly down on top of the cage, and then enter in search of food. Assuming that you have a clear view of the cage, you should then be able to close the door using the string, so as to catch the parrot within.

AILMENTS

Grey Parrots are normally healthy, long-lived birds, however, problems may arise on occasions. It is vital to never prolong action on a parrot (or indeed any other bird) to see if its condition improves. Veterinary advice should be sought as soon as you suspect something is wrong. This often makes the difference between a successful recovery, and a fatal outcome, since treatment can begin without delay.

Grey Parrots that are not feeling well will sit with their feathers fluffed and usually perch on two feet. A healthy bird will perch on one foot. Immediate veterinary care should be sought from the onset of these symptoms.

A bird's illness may be difficult for a veterinarian to diagnose. A thorough examination may be required, such as pictured here, where every aspect is checked.

THE SICK PARROT

The signs of illness in a parrot are reasonably obvious although accurate diagnosis is often far more difficult. Sick Greys tend to fluff up their feathers, and appear less active than normal. They may sleep huddled on the perch, with both feet gripping the wood for long periods during the day. Their appetite usually declines, and they may even refuse favorite items. Their eyes are often kept closed, and in some cases there may be a discharge from the eyes and the nostrils. The droppings alter in consistency, often becoming watery, and sometimes even blood-stained.

Recently imported parrots are probably most at risk to illness because of the dramatic change in their environment. You can reduce the risk of illness, however, by thoughtful care. Although the Greys will have undergone a period of quarantine, this does not mean that they are acclimatized. Such a bird should not be placed straight into an outside aviary.

In fact, Grey Parrots should only be placed in these quarters when the weather is warm, and

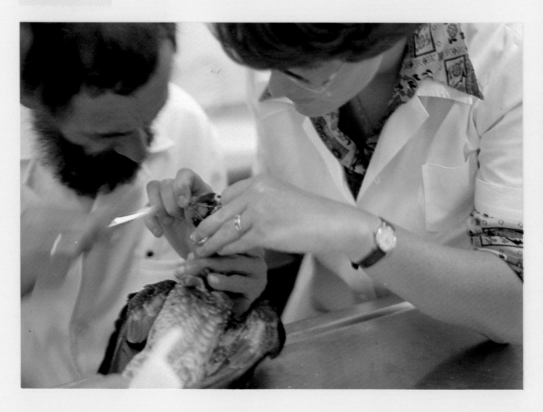

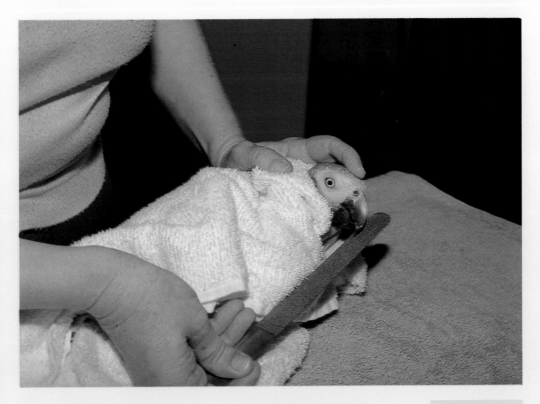

there is no risk of sudden cold, damp spells. It may even be advisable to bring the birds indoors for the following winter, housing them in a suitable flight until the spring. Similarly, if you have to transfer a parrot indoors in the winter time because it is ill, you will need to keep it inside until the weather is certain to remain warm again.

EMERGENCY CARE

It is always a good idea to be prepared in case one of your parrots falls ill. The necessary equipment is relatively inexpensive, and may prove invaluable in saving a Grey Parrot's life. Although you can purchase special heated hospital cages, these are usually too small to accommodate Greys successfully. Instead, obtain an infra-red lamp of the "dull-emitter" type because it emits heat rather than light. The lamp should be fitted into a reflector, which tends to concentrate the heat in the direction of the lamp. There should also be a variable heat controller, and possibly a clip to attach the unit to a cage, although you can rig up something quite easily, if required. It is a good idea

A Grey Parrot may, on occasion, require its beak trimmed. This is best if performed by an avian veterinarian or an experienced bird handler.

Preening is the means a Grey Parrot uses to clean itself. A bird can actually sit for hours going over each feather individually.

to set up the equipment and test it in advance. The lamp can be suspended either above the cage, or directed at one perch from the side. The parrot will then be able to sit in the warm rays from the lamp, or move to a cooler spot on the other perch. The temperature needs to be about 32°C (90°F) at its upper level. Be sure to keep the flex out of the reach of the parrot otherwise it might electrocute itself.

When sick, a Grey Parrot will often refuse to look for food in its quarters. You may tempt it by placing the perch down low and attaching a dish of seed next to it.

Seeds which have already been dehusked are useful under such circumstances. It is stocked by most health-food stores, and again, you may like to have a small quantity available. This type of seed is also valuable as a means of introducing young, hand-raised chicks to a more solid diet.

TREATING A SICK PARROT

When a bird appears sick, transfer it to a heated cage without delay. Watch as to how much seed and water it drinks. Often the fluid consumption of a parrot housed in these surroundings will rise, and this provides a useful means of treatment. A broad-spectrum antibiotic in the form of a powder, can then be dispensed via the drinking water, and into the parrot's body. Follow the dosage instructions very carefully with these drugs otherwise you may worsen your

parrot's condition. Change the solution twice a day, unless directed to the contrary by your veterinarian, since its potency is likely to decline.

In some cases, other methods of treatment may be necessary. Injections of an antibiotic, carried out by your veterinarian, can lead to a more rapid recovery, but there is the accompanying stress of handling a sick bird for this purpose.

Antibiotic tablets can also be useful, but the likely stress of administration is increased, as most Greys will refuse to swallow tablets unless they are placed right at the back

A pair of canine clippers may be used to clip a bird's nails. If unsure where to cut, ask your veterinarian to demonstrate for you.

Grey Parrots make wonderful and confiding pets. This Grey is so trusting that it is agreeing to being held on its back.

of the mouth. The beak must then be held for a few moments, to encourage the bird to swallow the medication.

These direct means of treatment ensure that your parrot receives a proper dose of the antibiotic. Administration via the drinking water is less reliable, since the parrot may not ingest a therapeutic dose. Often, a combination of methods, such as an injection linked with medicated water is recommended.

Your veterinarian will be able to advise you accordingly in a specific case, and can also arrange for any tests which may be necessary. Tests make it possible, for example, to discover which type of antibiotic is likely to be most effective against a particular bacterium.

SALMONELLOSIS

This is a disease caused by anaerobic bacteria which usually arises in Grey Parrots

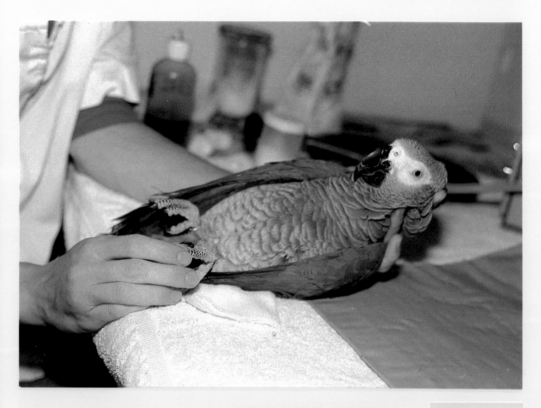

kept in unhygienic surroundings. It used to be a problem in some consignments of imported Greys, which presumably had drank contaminated water or ate bad seed. Now however, a vaccination is being used under these circumstances, and has dramatically reduced its incidence.

Problems can still arise in aviary surroundings if mice and other rodents are present, since they can spread the disease to parrots. Typically, a Grey Parrot suffering from salmonellosis appears very sick, passing liquid and sometimes blood-stained or dark brown feces. It often becomes unsteady on its feet, and is soon unable to perch.

Fluid and antibiotic therapy together may save an infected individual, but it then will be a hazard to other birds, as well as people, for a period of time. This is because the bacteria will still be present in the droppings. A careful program of monitoring is necessary to check that the infection is properly eliminated. Regular fecal sampling will be necessary for this purpose, since the *Salmonella* bacteria are

Your veterinarian knows the correct way to hold a parrot during a physical exam. In this fashion, the bird cannot struggle and is not being harmed at all.

This Grey Parrot has one wing clipped to prohibit it from flying. When done correctly, it is hardly noticeable.

usually excreted at intervals. One clear test will therefore not be a reliable indicator that the bird is actually clear of the disease.

Obviously, you will have to take sensible precautions when dealing with a parrot suffering from salmonellosis, as advised by your veterinarian.

Other bacterial diseases can be confused with salmonellosis, such as an E. coli infection. Once your parrot shows signs of recovery from a digestive disorder of this type it can be worthwhile adding live natural yogurt to its diet. Try smearing it lightly over a favored food, such as fruit. The yogurt contains beneficial bacteria which will help to repopulate the gut.

In the healthy parrot, the gut is lined with helpful bacteria. These help in preventing harmful bacteria from invading the body, and also make vitamins. Illness and antibiotics upset this delicate balance, and yogurt will help to combat this disturbance. There are also special *Lactobacillus* preparations which can be dispensed by your veterinarian.

These can be in powder form, and again can be administered by sprinkling over food.

CHLAMYDIOSIS (PSITTACOSIS)

This is the other disease of significance because it can be transmitted to people by sick parrots. Now, however, further studies have shown that many other animals including cats can be infected, and may also represent a threat to human health. For this reason, the disease itself is now more commonly known as chlamydiosis (being caused by *Chlamydia*

Filing a bird's nails is best achieved by wrapping the bird in a large, fluffy towel. This restricts the bird's movement, yet does not harm it.

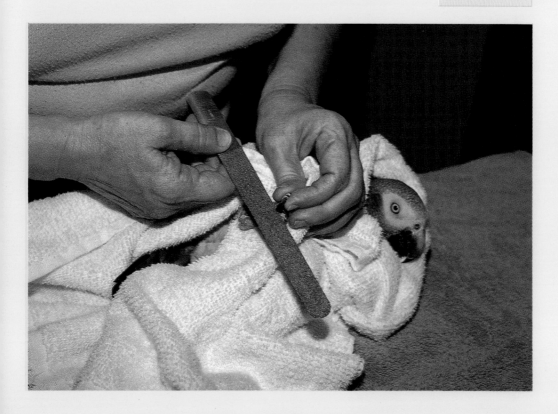

reason that you should always have birds that die submitted to a laboratory so an autopsy can be carried out. If by any chance chlamydiosis is discovered, then you can consult your doctor. The disease produces flu-like symptoms in humans but normally responds well to antibiotic therapy.

VIRAL DISEASE

It has become increasingly apparent, through recent research, that Greys as well as other parrots can sometimes develop viral diseases which affect the liver. Often there is no clear indication of a problem in acute cases. The bird apears unwell for a short time, and then dies rapidly. Again, autopsy findings should prove diagnostic. However, there is no effective treatment at present. Birds which do recover spontaneously often remain in poor health for the remainder of their lives because of permanent liver damage. This may be reflected by lack of activity and weight loss, with the parrot failing to make up this loss. No evidence exists to suggest this type of disease could be transmitted to people.

A perch or branch for a Grey Parrot should be of variable thickness. This will help to exercise the bird's feet, and naturally wear down the nails.

psittaci), than psittacosis, which suggests it is largely confined to parrots.

Medicating birds in quarantine with tetracycline in the food has meant that this disease is of little significance in terms of human health in North America. Similarly in Britain and elsewhere, quarantine restrictions mean that it can be diagnosed and treated if it does occur.

Signs of infection in parrots are not very clear, however, and post-mortem examinations are vital in the diagnosis of this disease. It is for this

Indeed, outbreaks are quite rare, and usually occur during a quarantine period. As in other cases, recently imported birds are most likely to be affected. A pair living on their own or a single Grey Parrot kept as a pet are most unlikely to encounter this type of disease.

EGG-BINDING

This condition only affects laying hens. Female birds, even those kept by themselves, will lay eggs when in breeding condition. It can, therefore, strike pet Greys kept without a mate when they begin to produce clutches of eggs. In this situation, the hen is unable to pass the egg, and it becomes stuck in her body. Various factors may be linked together in cases of egg-binding. The hen herself may be laying for the first time, or conversely could be old, so the muscular tone is not as effective as it would otherwise be under normal circumstances.

She may be short of calcium, causing the egg to have an incomplete shell, and her muscles cannot work properly when their calcium level is low. This appears to be the most common cause, since an injection of a calcium

compound given by a veterinarian will often resolve the problem effectively. Hens which choose to lay their eggs during cold weather are more at risk, because this also reduces muscular contractions. Egg-binding can strike at any stage during the laying of a clutch. Other possible causes include over-sized and mis-shaped eggs.

The symptoms are more obvious in a hen living in an aviary using a nest box,

The feathers of Grey Parrots are gray, edged with white, giving off a scalloped appearance.

Clear, bright eyes indicate good health. Ill birds will sit with their eyes half open and usually have some sort of discharge.

than they are in one kept as a pet. She will emerge from the box, appearing very unsteady on her feet. Her condition rapidly worsens, to the extent that she is unable to perch, and crouches on the floor. This is usually the effect of pressure from the trapped egg on a nerve, and it should pass once the egg is freed. If you suspect that a hen is egg-bound handle her gently. If the egg breaks inside her body it may well give rise to a fatal condition known as peritonitis. Keep her warm, under an infra-red lamp, and seek veterinary help without delay. This is an avian emergency, but once the egg is successfully removed, either naturally, after an injection, or by surgical means, she should undergo a full recovery. Do not encourage her to breed until the next year however, so that her body can recover. Look carefully at the diet, and if necessary, speak with your veterinarian about using a special soluble calcium and vitamin D_3 supplement.

A complication which may sometimes arise after egg-binding, particularly if the hen was straining to lay the egg for a considerable period before being discovered, is a prolapse of the oviduct. This will clearly be apparent, with pinkish tissue protruding through the anal opening. It needs to be cleaned and replaced without delay. It is best to ask your veterinarian for assistance. If necessary, a special temporary suture may have to be inserted here. This will hold the tissue back within the body until the inflammation declines and things rearrange themselves normally.

EYE INFLAMMATION

On occasions, Grey Parrots sometimes develop minor eye infections, possibly when scratching the

surrounding tissue. The eyelids swell up and close, and there may be a clear discharge from the eye. Treatment is usually quite straightforward, and involves applying either drops or an ointment to the affected eye approximately four times a day. It is important to treat the eye for the full period of time, as recommended by your veterinarian, in spite of the fact that an apparent recovery may be quite rapid. If you stop treating after a day or so, the infection may flare up again, and could prove less responsive to the treatment.

Although drops may be easier to apply, and will not stain the feathering on the head if misdirected, they tend not to penetrate as well as an ointment. Hold the parrot for a minute or so after treatment,

A supply of fresh food should always be available to your pet Grey at all times. They will eat small amounts of food all day long.

otherwise it may simply wipe the ointment off onto a convenient perch.

If both eyes are affected, however, this is usually indicative of a more serious infection. It could be linked with the nasal passages. Check the nostrils—they may be blocked, or a discharge could be evident here. This applies especially if the Grey in question already has an enlarged nostril, which tends to reflect a past history of infection in this area. Often, there are micro-organisms called mycoplasmas lurking here, which may not set up an infection by themselves, but if the bird is stressed in any way, even by a move to another aviary, more prominent signs of illness will appear.

Antibiotics may well be effective, although often they tend to subside rather than eliminate the infection. This may then re-emerge at intervals in the future. If the situation becomes necessary, your veterinarian may recommend more radical treatment such as administering an injection in this area. It may be worthwhile treating both members of a pair under these circumstances, as one bird may reinfect the other. As always, good hygiene is important. Be sure to clean out the nest box thoroughly if the birds roost here, as dust and droppings may also be implicated in such problems.

FEATHER-PLUCKING

Sadly, Grey Parrots are very susceptible to this vice, for which there is no easy cure. The reasons for such behavior are complex. Feather-plucking is worse in pet birds, kept on their own, and develops especially in older, mature individuals, over four years of age. This may reflect a frustrated desire to breed, coupled with other factors such as boredom (if the parrot is left on its own for long periods) and a poor diet. A lack of opportunity to bathe has already been mentioned, and needs to be taken into account.

In theory, there are feather parasites which could cause irritation and cause the bird to mutilate itself, but this appears exceedingly rare in cases which have been studied. In any event, you can purchase a special, safe aerosol to combat avian parasites from your pet store, and use as directed. This should kill any such parasites quite effectively. Although there is little risk of a pet bird, in particular, meeting further parasites

Opposite Page: **Feather-plucking can be caused by several things. The most common reasons are psychological. The bird may require to be stimulated in some way— more time away from its cage, new toys, new environment, or even a mate!**

Grey Parrots enjoy hot chili peppers. They carefully break these apart with their beaks and eat out the fiery seeds.

of this type, you could continue spraying the bird and its quarters every few months.

You will need to distinguish feather-plucking from a normal molt in the first instance. Feathers which are molted do not lead to bald patches, whereas feather-plucking leaves featherless areas, normally starting on the lower part of the chest. In bad cases, the Grey may continue pulling its feathers until virtually all accessible parts of the body are bald. The tail and flight feathers are usually left intact, however, the top of the wing is another favored area from which feathers are often pulled.

It is absolutely vital to try to act as soon as you see the early signs. Change the parrot's environment, possibly by moving it to another room. Increase its mental stimulation, by spending more time with it and letting it out into the room for longer periods. Buy new toys for your pet's cage—there are a number of excellent ones available from your local pet store. These are usually made from gnawable materials, and also provide the parrot with important minerals.

You can also purchase various preparations which are said to combat feather-plucking because of their foul taste on the plumage. These unfortunately are less reliable, although you may find an effective brand. It seems that because parrots do not have a highly-developed sense of taste, they are less likely to be deterred by this type of method than children who chew their fingernails!

If you can achieve a rapid cessation of the feather-plucking before too much damage results, you may find that it resolves itself. New plumage will grow, and hopefully this will not be removed as it emerges. This is the high risk period. Once a Grey Parrot, in particular, is semi-bald, it can be very difficult to persuade it to leave new feathers intact.

Should all else fail, then think seriously about either obtaining a mate for your pet, or seeking a new home for it where breeding facilities can be offered. Under these circumstances, your parrot's condition may improve, although there is a risk that it might slip back into its bad habits in the future.

Grey Parrots kept in aviaries are much less susceptible to feather-plucking. If it does arise under these circumstances, it may be that the dominant member of a pair is removing its partner's feathers. This applies if the back of the neck is affected. It is then really a symptom of excessive preening, often

Shiny objects will always catch the attention of your pet Grey. Be sure that no sharp metal objects are used as toys because these can cause harm to your pet.

A good wing stretch is one way a Grey Parrot is able to get its exercise. They may even begin to flap their wings several times to get the most of their exercise period.

just prior to the breeding season. If the hen is affected in this way, you may find that the plumage regrows uneventfully once the chicks have fledged.

The preen gland, located at the bottom of the back, just above the base of the tail, can also be involved in some cases of feather mutilation. It is here that the waterproofing oil is normally produced, and smeared over the parrot's plumage by its preening actions. Unfortunately, there may sometimes be a blockage of this gland. This can cause intense irritation, and affected parrots pick anxiously at this area, often with considerable vigor, removing feathers in the process. Contact your veterinarian, who should be able to overcome the problem by flushing the gland with a saline solution.

NEWCASTLE DISEASE

This is a viral disease that can devastate poultry flocks and can be introduced from parrots. For this reason, most countries impose quarantine restrictions on imported psittacines so that the disease can be contained if it is present on a shipment. If diagnosed, all birds are normally slaughtered. In its most severe form, Newcastle disease causes high mortality, with birds often displaying nervous symptoms prior to death.

OVERGROWN BEAKS AND CLAWS

Provided that your parrot has adequate opportunity to gnaw, then there should be little if any need to trim back the beak. In very old Greys, however, a slight malformation may occur. If left unchecked, this can develop to the extent that your parrot may have difficulty in eating. Cutting the beak back to shape is probably best left to an experienced avian veterinarian, since it is quite possible to cause bleeding if trimming is not carried out properly.

Some Greys occasionally have claws which grow at an abnormal angle, and these will need to be cut

The Grey Parrot is a very delicate eater. It will patiently remove the husks of seeds and nuts, and eat them one at a time.

Young Grey Parrots should be given a variety of branches to whittle away just as the adults receive.

back regularly, otherwise the parrot may become caught up in its quarters. Again, a veterinarian will undertake the task for you, or if you are careful, you could do this yourself. You will need a stout pair of nail clippers, as sold in pet stores and grooming parlors for dogs.

It is vital to check the blood supply to the claw before cutting it. Otherwise, if you cut it too short, it may bleed badly. The dark claws of Grey Parrots make the task harder, but in good light, you should see the darker streak which fades out before the end of the claw. You must then cut a short distance further down the nail, after the disappearance of the blood supply. The claw here should be dead, like a finger nail, and so will not bleed when it is cut.

Do seek proper advice before clipping the claw yourself. Should you by any chance cause slight bleeding, then a shaving pencil applied to the cut end will stimulate clotting.

PARASITES

Grey Parrots do not appear very prone to parasites, but it is sensible to use an avian aerosol as suggested

previously to kill any lice and mites, before releasing the birds into an aviary. You may also want to deworm them. Ask your veterinarian for advice. It is possible to test fecal samples to see if the eggs of such parasites are present, and then carry out treatment accordingly.

TUMORS

It is not surprising that Grey Parrots succumb with tumors, although they are not especially common. Older birds are most likely to be affected, and the signs depend very much on the area of the body concerned. Pet Greys are most at risk to lipomas, which are benign swellings of fatty tissue, often on the breast. It may be possible to remove these successfully by surgery, although recurrences are not uncommon.

Malignant (cancerous) tumors are less conspicuous. Weight loss is often the first obvious sign of their presence, and obviously the parrot's condition deteriorates.

Grey Parrots are inquisitive creatures and love to play. One favored toy can keep them amused for hours!

ONE LAST WORD

Young Grey Parrots have dark irises that become lighter as they mature.

ACCLIMATING YOUR PET GREY

The way in which a Grey Parrot acclimates itself depends upon several factors. Birds that have been domestically bred and hand-reared will adjust much sooner than those which have been previously owned, and previously owned birds will adjust quicker than imports.

You must be fully aware of the past history of your new pet Grey. The age of the bird can only be known for sure if

it is under five months old. At this age, the irises will still be dark in color, as discussed previously. Once the irises have turned white, it is rather difficult to guess the age, and one must rely on the seller's word.

If you are acquiring a hand-reared baby, be sure that the bird is fully weaned. It would be wise to purchase some rearing food along with the bird because the stress of moving a recently weaned chick often causes it to stop eating. This poses a problem for the new owner, especially if he has never fed a youngster in this manner. Ask the seller to demonstrate for you the easiest way to feed the bird, should the need arise.

Once you are sure the bird is eating on its own, you may begin to socialize with the bird and have it become part of the family. Remember, this chick can live in excess of fifty years, so it will be an intimate part of your life.

Hand-reared chicks do not know what it means to be "wild." They have experienced nothing but coddling and nurturing from a human, from

Grey Parrot chicks are rather helpless. If hand-rearing chicks, remember that you are their sole provider for food and nourishment.

A nest box for a Grey Parrot must be of a substantial size. It must be large enough to house both parents and several chicks.

practically right out of the egg! They look for attention from their owner, and are fully dependant. A bird that has been hand-reared is a full-time commitment, it is not something that can be cast aside and left alone to simply be fed and cleaned. Careful consideration must be given prior to purchasing a bird of this type. The time and devotion that is put into a hand-reared chick will be repaid ten-fold.

A word of advice if you should acquire a bird that has been previously owned. It may be for a very genuine reason that the bird is being given up, such as the owner does not have the time to spend with the bird that it truly deserves, death of the owner, or a number of other legitimate reasons. On the other hand, one should be cautious about collecting a bird of this type. Very often, owners give up a bird because it is a screecher, feather picker, or biter. These habits are hard to break, and can discourage new owners to the point that they never want to have a bird again. It is important to ask

This Grey Parrot is being held for examination. Note the ease in which the chest, feet, under wings, head and eyes can be checked.

questions of the original owner, if possible, and be sure that you may return the bird for a full refund if any of these habits appear within a short period after acquiring.

Whenever a bird is moved from an environment it has been used to, it must be given a certain amount of time to readjust itself to its new surroundings. The best thing to do is to have the bird's cage all set up prior to its arrival. In this way one may just release the bird into its new cage the moment it comes home. The bird should then be left alone so that it may accustom itself to the cage, surrounding noises, and movements. Do not try to

handle the bird until you are sure that it has been eating well. Sometimes a new bird will not eat for a day or so after being moved, and handling it would only stress it more.

After the bird has been shelling its seed and eating, you may approach the cage, and allow the bird to become familiar with you. If it does not seem bothered by your presence, you may begin to handle it. Every bird's personality is different. Some take longer to adjust than others, and some will resent the fact that their original owners are gone. However, most tame birds that have been previously owned long for attention, and will only be

This is a typical shipping crate used when transporting birds.

Grey Parrots that are unaccustomed to humans will climb to the furthest corner of their cage to escape any possible danger.

too happy to have you handle them.

Imported birds must be accustomed to their new surroundings in a completely different way. They are very skittish and have been handled poorly by man in the past. Someone probably captured them from the wild, grabbed them with a glove, shoved them in a box, and then held them down to clip their wing and inoculate them during quarantine.

Quarantine stations are filled with birds and few employees. This means that the birds are fed in a harried way and no attention is given to them before they leave.

These birds usually cower in a corner of the cage and are rather frightened. They require a lot of patience and tender loving care. Handling a bird of this type does not come quick or easy. Much time will be involved just in getting the bird to feel secure. Be patient! This type of bird will make an excellent pet, and will grow to trust you just as the other types.

The nominate subspecies *(erithacus)* of the Grey Parrot, *P. erithacus.* The other subspecies is known as *Psittacus erithacus timneh* (opposite page), the Timneh Grey Parrot. The most noticeable differences between the two are the darker tail and lighter upper mandible of the Timneh.

HANDBOOK OF MACAWS
DR. A.E. DECOTEAU

THE WORLD OF MACAWS

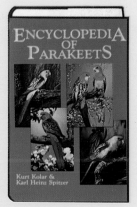

ENCYCLOPEDIA OF PARAKEETS
Kurt Kolar & Karl Heinz Spitzer

H-1044; 97 full-color photos and 37 black and white.

H-1079; over 70 full-color photos.

H-1094; contains many full-color photos.

PARROTS

A Beginner's Guide to Parrots

PARROTS
A COMPLETE INTRODUCTION

Your First PARROT
Martin Gabin

KW-032; 47 full color photos 21 black and white.

T-109; completely illustrated with full-color photos.

CO-028S; 108 full-color photos.

YF-113; illustrated throughout with many full-color photos.

Parrots And Related Birds

A STEP-BY-STEP BOOK ABOUT PARROTS

H-912; 160 color photos.

SK-031; over 50 full color photos and drawings.

Parrots of the World
Joseph M. Forshaw
William T. Cooper

PS-753; almost 300 large color plates plus many line illustrations.

T.F.H. offers the most comprehensive selections of books dealing with pet birds. A significant collection of titles is presented here; they and the thousands of other animal books published by T.F.H. are available at the same place you bought this one, or write to us for a free catalog.

SUGGESTED READING

KW-018; 41 full color photos, 45 black and white.

PS-780; illustrated throughout with full-color photos, maps and charts.

KW-025; full color drawings and photos throughout.

KW-039; illustrated with full-color photos and drawings.

PS-781; full color photos throughout.

T.F.H. Publications One
T.F.H. Plaza Third & Union
Avenues Neptune, NJ 07753

PS-761; 83 full-color photos, 39 black and white.

T-101; full-color photos throughout.

CO-008S; 56 full-color photos, 52 drawings.

SK-002; features full-color photos or drawings on every page.

KW-070; completely illustrated w/ photos and drawings throughout.

PR-003; completely illustrated with full-color photos.

The World's Largest Publisher of Pet Books

H-1093; contains many full-color photos.

CO-004S; 94 full-color photos and 18 drawings.

H-964; 304 black and white photos, 99 color.

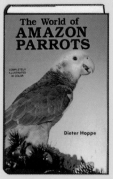

PS-839; 74 full-color photos, 10 black and white.

TT-007; filled with beautiful full-color photos.

H-1072; over 100 photos

PS-801; Over 30 full-color photos, 20 black and white.

T-103; full-color photos throughout.

CO-012S; Full-color photos, and drawings throughout.

PS-743; 60 full-color photos 108 black and white.

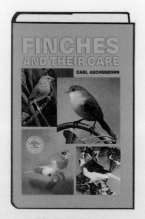

TS-159; contains almost 200 full-color photos.

TS-107; 200 full-color photos.

PS-797; 50 full color photos

TU-005; full-color photos throughout.

TS-140; 97 full-color photos.

TW-105; completely illustrated with full-color photos and drawings.

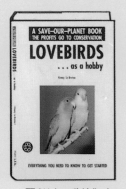

TT-011; beautiful full-color photos throughout.

H-1040; 117 full color photos.

TS-155; 180 full-color photos and drawings.

T.F.H. books are bound to last.

INDEX

Page numbers in **boldface** refer to illustrations.

Grey Parrots often enjoy the company of another bird. They should not, however, be housed in the same cage with a bird of another species. Under your watchful eye they may be left to play together.